STOP WOI

START
LIVING

NATIONAL LIBRARY OF CANADA CATALOGUING IN PUBLICATION DATA

Nahirny, Dianne
Stop working . . . start living : how I retired at 36

ISBN 1-55022-484-0
1. Retirement income. 2. Early retirement. 3. Retirement — Planning. 1. Title.
NG179.N34 2001   332.024'01   C2001-900810-4

Cover and text design by Tania Craan
Cover photo by Rob Allen
Layout by Mary Bowness

Printed by Webcom

Distributed in Canada by
General Distribution Services,
325 Humber College Blvd.,
Toronto, ON, M9W 7C3

Published by ECW PRESS
2120 Queen Street East, Suite 200
Toronto, ON, M4E IE2
ecwpress.com

This book is set in Futura and Garamond.
PRINTED AND BOUND IN CANADA

The publication of *Stop Working . . . Start Living* has been generously supported by
the Canada Council, the Ontario Arts Council, and the Government of Canada
through the Book Publishing Industry Development Program. **Canadä**

Disclaimer
This publication is designed to provide accurate and authoritative information. It is sold with
the understanding that the publishers are not engaged in rendering legal, accounting or other
professional advice. If legal advice or other expert assistance is required, the services of a com-
petent professional should be sought. The analysis contained herein represents the experiences
and opinions of the author, but the author and publisher are not responsible for the results of
any actions taken on the basis of information in this work nor for any errors or omissions.

STOP WORKING...

START LIVING

HOW I RETIRED AT THE AGE OF 36...
WITHOUT WINNING THE LOTTERY

DIANNE NAHIRNY

ECW PRESS

For Peter and Tatianna, Fred and Anna, and Mary

This book wouldn't have been written if it hadn't been for the following:

John and Julie. Without them, my life, my lifestyle, and my book would never have come into being. They are my inspiration.

Mark and Jane, for their expert advice, generous assistance, and encouragement.

Sandie. Many times I might have given up if it hadn't been for her unwavering belief in me, and all her help.

Jack, for recognizing my potential and patiently guiding me along.

STOP WORKING . . . START LIVING

CHAPTER ONE

GET RICH QUICK

This is a "get rich quick" book with a promise. It really *is* possible to retire early, even though today's money experts would have you believe there are no quick schemes that work, you must invest over the long term, and you will need an unbelievably huge amount saved when you finally do retire. I've proven them wrong. I didn't follow conventional wisdom, and I have achieved financial freedom. My promise is to show how you can too.

The average person will spend more than 30 years working before retirement even becomes a possibility. I earned a mediocre wage and made financial mistakes along the way, yet I retired in half that time. Depending on your own circumstances, you could retire much sooner than I did. But regardless of timing, to become financially free, all you need to do is follow my example.

I've always questioned conventional wisdom. How many financial advisors do you know who are comfortably retired in their mid-30s? Are they retired, rich, and young? To me, "retired" means having all the time in the world and the freedom to choose how to spend it. "Rich" means being free from debt, having all living expenses covered, continually satisfying desires, and enjoying luxuries to the fullest. "Quick" is the freedom to retire young. All this is not only possible but also sustainable. I should know — I've done it.

You probably wouldn't notice me walking down the street, and you wouldn't pick me out in a crowd. Just like the majority of the millionaires in North America (according to *The Millionaire Next Door*), I look like every other ordinary person in your neighbourhood, probably a little happier but a perfectly average woman — except that I'm retired, young, and rich.

I spend my time however I choose. If I want to sleep in, I do. If I don't want to go out in the cold or rain, I don't. There really isn't much that can't wait until another day. Usually, I get up around 9 a.m. unless I was up late the night before finishing a gripping novel or watching a video into the early hours. I have a breakfast of home-baked cinnamon bread, freshly squeezed juice, and tea out on the patio, weather permitting. Otherwise, it's breakfast on a white wicker tray in bed to enjoy with the newspaper, a magazine, or a television show. After breakfast and a leisurely shower, I dress to suit myself. Then I consider what I feel like doing that morning — perhaps looking over my investment portfolio, possibly tending my garden, maybe going for a hike down the ravine or taking a stroll to the library. Then I may meet family or friends for lunch, and in the afternoon I may delve into a project of personal interest. Later, an art class, yoga, ballet, or aerobic exercise provides a nice break. I also choose "work" as a part of most days, but not for the income. It can be an enjoyable hobby, a new project that could generate some cash, or helping out as a volunteer. Working for fun, for personal satisfaction, to socialize, or to help others isn't really "work" at all. My evenings and weekends are filled with trips to antique markets and auctions, watching amateur theatre productions, attending investment seminars, meeting with the area garden club, or even just reading and puttering around the house.

My neighbours watched the gradual renovations made recently to my Tudor-style house, and along with the congenial nods of approval I could see the curiosity in their eyes. They seemed to ponder my situation: *I was always at home. I was young and on my own. Didn't I have a job to go to? How could I be making all these home improvements without one? Didn't I need a job?* I could only imagine their speculations.

Then one Saturday morning, as I was re-sealing my driveway, a neighbourhood couple stopped to admire my efforts and chat. Inevitably, they asked the question that finds its way into polite conversation: "Where do you work?" I still have trouble answering that question. "I don't work" has all the wrong connotations, and it's untrue — I work, but only within my areas of personal interest. "I don't need to work" sounds arrogant. It reminds me of a snobbish character in the short story *Any Reasonable Offer* by Kurt Vonnegut. When asked what he does for a living, the man answers, "Do? Why, whatever amuses me. . . ." Instead, I answer, "Actually, I'm retired." The response is usually surprised silence followed by "Oh, it must be nice!" And it is. Really nice. I think everybody should retire young, and I'm going to show you how.

I believe almost anyone can do what I've done. It doesn't matter whether you're just starting out, single, or married with or without children, and it doesn't even matter how much you earn. There are benefits and drawbacks in every situation. What you do with what you have is all that really counts.

Early retirement doesn't necessarily mean never working again; rather, it means being able to freely choose the amount, if any, and type of work to pursue. During my retirement, I've been approached a few times to fill temporary vacancies as a favour, and I've been happy to oblige. The jobs have always been new and different. When the head librarian at my neighbourhood branch asked me if I'd be interested in working a few hours a week, I gladly joined the library staff. Although initially I worked 12 hours a week, I was able to reduce the number of hours to just Monday mornings when I wanted more time to spend on a hobby. What made each job fun, however, is that it wasn't a necessity. Whether you want to have any kind of job or not will depend on your own definition of retirement.

In writing this book, I'm pleased to prove by example that early retirement is possible for almost anyone. I also promise to present my formula for success in an enjoyable and concise manner. Since I've found many personal finance books to be heavy reading, I tried to create a money book in a "short notes" style, condensing concepts to their simplest forms. A fast and to-the-point read is no less educational or useful than one padded with extraneous information. I'll show you how

I became financially independent simply, and you'll learn how to apply the same principles to your set of circumstances for your own ultimate success.

This book is for all those who wonder how I could possibly have done it. It's also for everyone who seriously thinks there must be some explanation other than careful planning and determined action for my early retirement. As well, it's for those believers who know there's a way; they just need to be shown how.

My freedom was not financed by a winning lottery ticket, inheritance, gift, government subsidy, or financial settlement of any kind. Actually, I should be among the "working poor," slaving away at a low-paying job, living in a low-rent apartment. I've never had the wedding gifts (down payment on a house, cash, new appliances and/or furniture) that many couples receive. Likewise, there hasn't been any help from in-laws. My parents didn't give me the money. I never had the benefit of a two-income household (two people really can live more cheaply than one!), and, as a single employed person, I have had few tax breaks. Over my 15-year working life, I averaged a gross salary of about $20,000 a year. And while I've always lived on my own, living poorly has never been my idea of financial freedom. I'm not a "back to the land" person either, choosing voluntary simplicity over central air conditioning, a dishwasher, or packaged food. I live in the city, and I like to live well.

A middle-class lifestyle complete with luxuries is how I have chosen to live. Travelling by Concorde, acquiring antiques, and enjoying the arts are a part of it. I also spend time on various other hobbies, I volunteer, and I visit more often now with family and friends. I vacation as I please. I enjoy the picturesque walk to the shops and library along the upscale avenues of manicured lawns and charming homes where I live. I take in the local sights, and I take it easy.

So how did I manage to own a home with all the "toys" and enjoy a comfortable retirement lifestyle when most people my age aren't even at the starting gate?

I have not been a stockbroker, accountant, or financial advisor. I did not start out with any special knowledge, but I believe my childhood environment provided the basic skills, and my interest in personal finance books contributed as well. I've found both good and bad advice and have made my share of mistakes. But those experiences have paved the road to financial independence. Even after some money blunders, I still retired very early — and so can you.

You will need perseverance. I'm an impatient person and stubbornly go after what I want until I find a way to get it. While this isn't one of the best qualities for building a happy relationship, it has helped me in my quest for a quick and easy path to financial freedom. Throughout the years, my goal was always with me. Determination was a necessary component of my success, along with knowing what to do and how to do it. For you, it should be easier, and could take less time, since this book not only shows the route to early retirement but also points out the roadblocks that can occur and how to detour around them. I've already done the thinking and rethinking, the mistakes and learning, and the trying and practising. All you have to do is read this book and put the principles to work.

I present the method in two parts, showing first what you need to do and then how you actually do it. The first part, "The Plan," introduces the basic financial concepts I learned when I was young and then the steps I took as an adult that led to my financial independence. The second part, "The Procedure," provides the means for putting my plan into action and moulding it to your own situation, with practical suggestions and techniques.

If you're single, earn a low income (my average salary for the first three years was $15,000), and stay single over the next 10–15 years, you have the potential to retire at the end of that time. I'm living proof. Depending on your circumstances, if you're not just starting out, or you're earning a much better income, or you're married (with or without children), you could also retire within that time frame or sooner. You may already have your household furnishings and appliances, car, mortgage partly paid off, or even some investments and retirement funds saved. Your children may be young, entering university, or leaving home, or you may be childless. It doesn't matter. Every situation will be different, including income and debt levels. These factors will not keep you from ultimately succeeding, but how you choose to deal with them will affect the timing of your retirement. If you want financial freedom, it's entirely up to you. If you'd rather tend your garden than look after your customers, you can. If you'd rather lounge in your backyard than doze in a traffic jam, you can. If you'd rather go hiking than sit through a business meeting, you can.

You *can* reach financial independence without feeling deprived, just as I have. But it takes conscious living. You may have to adopt a new attitude toward your use of money and exchange some bad habits for good ones. You may need to make some decisions about your lifestyle and prioritize the things you truly value in life.

Simply put, you get rich quick by accelerating the accumulation of assets and the elimination of liabilities. To continue indulging in your dreams, you keep building your asset base, even after you've retired. Be encouraged, though, that doing so will be easier if you follow the guidelines in this book. Other money books have you performing long calculations with schedules that resemble tax returns (as if you'd really want to do *that* in your spare time), and by filling out questionnaires, charts, and budgets you'll supposedly benefit monetarily sometime in the future. Then there are books that assume you already have a sizeable amount of cash and only need advice on how to invest it. Still others are dissertations on the psychology of money. The books identify, label, analyse, and discuss all the possible behaviours that characterize an individual's view of money. How this approach gets people off the couch and on their way to better finances I don't know. It wouldn't work for me.

So get ready for an easy read — simple and fast ways to stop working and start living. Immediately after putting this book to work, you'll feel freer, more secure, more retired! If you take action and persevere, you won't have to suffer the seemingly interminable wait until conventional retirement, and you'll avoid the common, shocked response "I'll have to save how much?" While other books offer difficult, plodding methods to achieve financial security, this book offers the techniques simply, with as little hassle or drudgery as possible. Plain and simple. Faster and easier. So what are you waiting for?

CHAPTER TWO

CHILDREN'S PROGRAMS

THE FORMATIVE YEARS

I feel very fortunate that my home environment provided me with the beginning necessary for a future of financial independence. My father started out in radio and TV repair, so our house was the first on the block to have a colour television. My brother and I thought this was good fortune in itself, but the kind of children's programming that contributed to my freedom wasn't the kind on TV. The use of money had important consequences in our household, and it influenced our everyday life. It's not that my parents directly set out to teach me their money philosophy — I was a captive audience, and being impressionable I couldn't help but absorb their gems of financial wisdom. I listened, observed, and followed the rules, completely unaware of the beneficial foundation being built around me.

"Teach your children well" was a line in a popular song when I was growing up, and the money concepts I learned from family interactions have served me well. One of my earliest recollections is of my European grandfather towering over me and demanding to know "What for you need this one?" I have no idea now what the item was, but the point was clear: there were needs, and there were wants. This concept repeated itself regularly through parental idioms such as "You don't need it," "We give you everything you need," and "Money doesn't grow on trees." Sometimes, when my father was in a teasing mood, he would let me think I might get what I was pleading for. He would pose the same question as my grandfather but phrase it differently. One time, he said, "Suppose you tell me exactly why you need an 'X'."

That was the bait. I didn't know that my dad was only doing this for sport and that, really, I didn't stand a chance of ever getting my coveted 'X'. I was so easily led. Perking up with hope, I answered too quickly, "Because I want it."

My father countered, "No, I asked you to tell me why you *need* it, not want it." After seeing my crestfallen face, he continued, "But go ahead, tell me why you want it," and he kept the game going.

"Because I really like it," I answered.

"That's not a good enough reason. Try again," he teased.

"Because all my friends have one."

I think everyone knows the old "If all your friends jumped off a bridge . . ." wisecrack I heard next.

Finally, my mother ended my suffering by shaming my father with "Stop teasing her! You know she takes you seriously." I remember Dad slinking out of the room, leaving me standing there and wondering what had happened.

When my parents were busy, whining was countered with "Because I said so" and "Don't talk back," immediately followed by some sort of punishment if it didn't stop. I became very well behaved. Whether these parenting skills are considered politically correct today really isn't the point. The real point was well made: need versus want.

My parents controlled how money was spent simply because they were the source of it. If they didn't work, they didn't have it. But equally important, money didn't control them. They were never "work slaves" since they chose the type and duration of work freely. They still enjoy "working" as long as it's at endeavours of their own choosing. My parents started out with little, but they quickly attained a comfortable, secure lifestyle in their own way. They had control over income, spending, saving, and ultimately their destiny.

The lesson in our home was that you only got something if you worked for it. Working meant making something or doing something that someone else would pay for. While my parents covered all my needs, and I had a privileged childhood with lessons, many vacations, special-occasion gifts, and a lot of quality family time, there were still all those unlimited wants every child has. (Only much later did I realize that wants are limitless throughout life.) And they were of the utmost importance to me. Even though I had the usual chores, I didn't have an allowance. I was so envious of my friends who were handed money weekly to spend as they pleased. If I wanted anything from my wish list, I had to use the concept of exchanging something of value for money. This became one of the most important lessons in helping me to achieve financial independence. There really are no free lunches. Whatever I got was all up to me.

So how does a kid in grade school earn money? As it turned out, my parents provided a great example. Exchanging value for money took on many forms. My mother sold real estate and ran an office. My father was an entrepreneur mainly, but he started out working for an employer and then quickly went into sales. Those were his day jobs. Other endeavours included home building and renovating, but everyday opportunities also provided spare cash.

While my father was working at an appliance repair shop, a woman had her washing machine brought in to be fixed, but she decided the estimate was too high. She also refused to pay the charge to deliver it back to her house. No one at the store wanted the machine, so my father took it home, repaired it, and then sold my mother's old wringer washer. The couple who bought it didn't have a car, so they were happy the wringer had casters. Laughing at themselves, they wheeled it down the street, around the corner, and presumably all the way home.

Another time my father won a new television in a contest, so my parents placed an ad in the paper to sell our old one. It had a real wood cabinet but needed some TLC. I was paid to clean it up, fill in the scratches, and polish the wood to a fine shine. A man called for the details and came by when just my mother and I were at home. He liked the TV but turned to my mother seriously and said, "Lady, are you sure your husband knows you're selling this?" After questioning her a few more times, he bought it and carried it hurriedly out of our house. Even in the driveway with the TV safely in his car, he kept glancing down the street, wary of my father's untimely arrival.

At my father's renovation projects, I swept and cleaned to make some pocket money. At one house, I agreed to razor scrape and then clean the multipaned, leaded-glass windows. I was up on a ladder in the hot sun for hours, scraping off old paint and wiping each tiny, diamond-shaped pane clean. Finally, when the job was done, I worked out my earnings to be about one dollar an hour. The money wasn't worth the effort I spent, and I never did windows for my father again. What I gleaned from all this, however, is that a product or service that someone else wants can be exchanged for money. I also learned, though, that the exchange is not always fair and that the amount of money paid doesn't always equal the amount of work done. It was a valuable lesson that I applied to my future jobs.

I soon found easier ways to earn money. I started making velvet bookmarks with customized designs and sold them at school. After a Sunday fishing trip with my brother and Dad, I took a crayfish to school for "show and tell" and promptly sold it to a boy in my class. Unfortunately, when he put it in the aquarium at home, his sister watched in horror as the crayfish immediately snipped off the tails of her goldfish and dined on their helpless bodies. A few days later, he brought the crayfish back in for "show and tell," this time laid out in a match box, its stiffened form shellacked for all eternity.

Another way to earn money was looking for pop bottles to return for the deposit. Some of the bottles came from my grandparents' basement. On one occasion, I found a bottle with the tortured remains of a large bug inside, frozen in its pre-deceased position of reaching up toward the opening. Alarmed,

I ran upstairs with it. My grandmother tried to calm me down. Explaining to me, she chuckled: "He go in, he not go out. You see? — bug catcher!" Then she roared with laughter at the bug's comeuppance. Old Country humour, I guess. I didn't get it. And, as for that bottle, I decided to leave it behind.

My brother and I made regular contributions to the local newspaper's Junior Press Club. Our work wasn't always published, but often enough we won gift certificates from a major department store. It was worth the time and effort, and the coupons could be converted into cash at Mom's Bank.

At other times, I was told to "just look around" and find ways of exchanging something of value for money. My parents had an extensive garden and a big thicket of raspberries lining the backyard. When the berries were ripe, I was allowed to pick them and sell quarts to neighbours as long as I went door to door myself. At my shy hesitation, my mother would say "You've got a voice — use it!" just as her mother had said to her when she was a child. My grandparents couldn't speak English well, and they needed my mother to communicate for them when dealing with others. That phrase, however, was instrumental in driving away my shyness. Not only was I able to sell produce to the neighbours, but I also discovered another way of helping them to part with their money. The idea came from the teachers at grade school who urged the students to collect money for various charities by going door to door. No problem for me: I already had experience doing that with raspberries. But after talking it over with a girlfriend, we decided that a front like that would be a great way to get money for us! My friend never lacked confidence, so we decided to try our idea on an elderly lady a few houses down the street. She was very nice when we told her we were collecting money for school, but then she wanted to know which charity it was for. We really hadn't thought about it, so after stumbling around a bit we just said we couldn't remember. I think she knew what we were up to, and I was surprised when she went back into the house and returned with a handful of change. We eagerly took the money and skipped back to my house. But our elation was short-lived. My mother was waiting at the front door with her arms crossed; she had somehow managed to witness the whole escapade. I quickly recognized that she had a voice too, and she used it on us. She made us march right back to that sweet elderly lady to return all her money, and rightly so. By then, I knew what we had done was wrong. It was also my first big lesson in financial risk management. Easy money has its risky side — you can win big, but be prepared to lose it all and suffer the consequences. I went back to selling berries.

The garden was such a good source of food that my parents jumped on the "homegrown" bandwagon and registered me and my brother for children's garden plots at the nearby Botanical Gardens. I hated going there, even though I won a few prizes for my garden. I think the prizes were really for Mom's weeding skills. Both my parents were thrilled at the amount of produce the whole family now generated, and they bought a freezer for the yearly bounty. Labels of "The Midnight Canning Company" appeared on the jars in the pantry and the containers in the freezer. One year produced such a bumper crop of yellow beans that we ate them every single night for a whole winter. To this day, I will not touch yellow beans, and I can't for the life of me understand how my parents could stand them at every supper. "We eat whatever we grow," they said. Pride perhaps? The fact is, growing our own vegetables was not only a cheap source of food but also a good education. As an adult, I've enjoyed the benefits of a garden for years, although you will never catch me planting yellow beans.

The garden was also an example of saving money. There were two ways of generating savings: by spending less on what was bought and by setting aside income. Those two acts resulted in money in the bank. This concept was a given in our household. "You have to save!" was equal in importance to "You have to brush your teeth!" and said in the same manner as expressing shock that anyone could ever think otherwise. The garden saved us the money that would have been spent at the market or the grocery store (less the minimal cost of seeds) for the same food.

My first bank account was set up for me a few weeks after I was born. All my relatives came to visit and gathered around the bassinet. Fortunately for me, when my grandfather looked in, I gave him such a big smile that he rewarded me handsomely. Pulling out his wallet, he declared, "$20! I give $20 for her smile — for my granddaughter!" So began my savings. My mother regularly added the baby bonus cheques to that account as well. As I grew up and received earnings or gifts of money, I was strongly encouraged to deposit at least half of each amount in the bank. Saving money by spending less was a more abstract concept, yet it also resulted in savings by default. I learned that I could save money by not buying something in the first place or by spending the least possible amount on it.

We also saved money by not automatically replacing every worn or broken item. First we'd judge if the item was really needed or even still wanted; then we'd decide whether to fix it, borrow one, or buy a new one. That is not to say we didn't have anything new. My parents did buy new items, but for things that didn't matter that much, well, why buy new? We weighed value (price of an item) against effort (income to buy it) in deciding how worthwhile something was. My parents always thought about the trade-offs before making a purchase. Add the importance of savings and you realize how unimportant paying the highest price for almost anything really is.

Savings were used to get rid of debt, which in my parents' case was the mortgage on the family home. There was no car loan or any other kind of consumer debt. My parents believed that, if they couldn't pay for something in cash, they couldn't afford it. Rather than borrow money, they saved money until they had enough for whatever they wanted; today this is known as the seemingly archaic concept of delayed gratification.

My father, who enjoyed horseback riding on occasion, made the mistake of introducing it to me. It started with pony rides, and as I got older we spent quality time together on trail rides. Naturally, I wanted my own horse, and, while my parents could have bought one for me, they decided against it. So it was my responsibility to satisfy my want on my own. Realistically, I knew I couldn't buy and board a horse, and all I really wanted was to ride one, not to own and look after one. Riding lessons, though, were within my grasp. I asked for lessons instead of other gifts, and I did extra chores around the house for money. I added half of my babysitting income and paycheques from after-school jobs at a gift shop and the public library. Naturally, the other half went into savings.

Besides delayed gratification, other solutions were either to buy an item used or to make it yourself. I got new figure skates one Christmas, but when I outgrew them the next year my mother decided to buy me used ones. Through a friend, she bought a used pair in my new size and in good condition, but they were a pastel blue. I can't say I was fond of the colour, but they were good skates, and no one stole them.

As a family, we travelled to Florida every other year in the spring, and we went camping for summer holidays before we had our summer house. I regularly went fishing with my dad and brother, but I really just wanted to be in the rowboat that my father had made. It seems to me now that he made a lot of our worldly goods, but I suppose if he could build a house he could build almost anything.

My grandmother was an expert seamstress and passed along her skills to my mother. When I was little, she made beautiful clothes — lovely suits for herself and cute outfits for me. Evening classes enhanced her professionalism. When I was a preteen, she encouraged my ideas and gave me final approval on any clothes she sewed for me. When we went to fabric stores, it was fun searching the notions department for tapestry, ribbon, silk cord, and feather trims. I was getting too tall for a favourite blue dress of mine, so my mother let me add a row of matching blue feathers to lengthen the bottom. She also let me choose fake leopard fur for the lining, collar, and cuffs on a coat she was making for me. My own attempts at sewing clothes were average at best, but I've always done my own tailoring, thanks to Mom's teachings.

Heavy draperies, curtains, and sheers in the house were also my mother's handiwork. The curtains in the kitchen had tiebacks that were formerly a multicoloured plastic chain belt that my mother and I shared. The belt happened to match the colours in the curtains perfectly. My father took an upholstery course and recovered our first sofa and chair, which became my brother's "bachelor pad" furniture and later my first living room suite. Led by my parents' example, we took good care of our things and saved our money.

Hand-me-downs were normal, and I was too young to know that my wagon, snowsuit, and skis were originally my brother's. They were in excellent condition and perfectly fine for me.

While growing up, I realized that it was somewhat unusual for a family to be so self-sufficient. I discovered that people hired decorators to paint and wallpaper their houses or contractors to pour a patio, build a garage, or do other remodelling work. I remember asking my father once how he was able to do so many things (and everything was always done well). He said, simply, "I learned." After more prodding, he admitted that his father had taught him many building skills, and he had taken practical subjects in high school and later do-it-yourself night-school courses. He also learned from his work and read many how-to books. Similarly, my mother became an expert in many areas simply by learning (courses, books, friends, and family) and practising her skills.

I enjoyed the material benefits of their industriousness, but

I also questioned their lifestyle. It seemed to take an awful lot of time and effort. What I didn't realize then were the financial benefits of choosing self-sufficiency. Their lifestyle gave them a huge head start in achieving security and freedom.

I wanted to have control over my destiny, just like my parents did over theirs. So my goal of early retirement and my determination to meet that goal started early in life, when most teenagers were thinking about future career possibilities. My parents believed that a university education was the best option, and the pressure was on to choose high school courses that would complement my future university discipline. That fateful discussion with my father went something like this:

Dad: "Do you know what you're going to want to do with your life?"

Me: "Not exactly." (I was 14!)

Dad: "You're going to have to narrow it down. There are two basic areas for the professions: science and math. You could be a doctor, engineer, lawyer, or chartered accountant. You won't take biology, so that leaves out doctor, and you didn't like physics, so that leaves out engineering. You could still be a lawyer or a C.A."

Me: "Do I really have to go through all that university and become either of those? I'll probably get married and have a family, anyway. Until then, what about art? Singing, dance, and art are my favourites."

Dad: "The arts are fine for a hobby, but you can't expect to earn a good income in that area, and you may never get married, so you will have to think about being able to support yourself. What else do you like?"

Me: "Money."

Dad: "Well, yes. Then how about accounting? You could be an actuary or a C.A."

Great. Something to look forward to. It was my first realization of the unpleasant things to come. By the process of elimination, and the encouragement of my well-meaning parents, I was to become a number cruncher.

FIRST STEPS

- Recognize the difference between needs and wants.
- Be aware that wants are limitless.
- Control money — don't let it control you.
- Money is only a medium of exchange: you get it or give it for something of value.
- Value basically equals time and/or effort.
- Time and effort are precious limited resources.
- Risk must be assessed in any financial exchange.
- The act of saving is omnipotent.
- Savings are generated in two ways:
  - paying out the least for the most; and
  - keeping a high percentage of all sources of income.
- Practise delayed gratification: first earn, then spend.

CHAPTER THREE

THE STUDENT YEARS

W hile I didn't like what university had in store for me, I was resigned to the fact that nevertheless I'd be going. In the meantime, I still had a couple of years of high school to come up with a secret plan of action to circumvent the career and accomplish early retirement. That was both a need and a want.

Since I'd already learned that needs and wants can be satisfied with money, I thought I would simply need enough money to live the lifestyle I had become accustomed to, with added luxuries, of course. I would need money to cover the most important basics first: a place to live and food. Then I'd need additional money for "everything else." It wasn't much of a secret plan, but it was a start, and I had time on my side to solve the problem of getting the required funds without having to endure years of being the dreaded chartered accountant or actuary.

What I really needed were answers, which meant doing

research. Whenever my parents wanted to do something, they simply found out how to do it and then tried it themselves. Ignorance is bliss, and as a teenager I believed anything I wanted to do was as easy as that. You just learned how, and then you did it yourself. The trouble was, I didn't know any self-made wealthy people to ask, and I couldn't seek help from my parents because they thought my future plans were set. In the 1970s, there weren't nearly as many financial planning seminars as there are now, but even if there were I couldn't have gone to them secretly. All I could do was observe the money-handling skills of my parents and read their books. Fortunately, they enjoyed reading about personal finance, and their collection was a bonanza! Great titles such as *The Money Game, Crisis Investing, Smart Money Shortcuts to Becoming Rich, How to Live Rich when You're Not, Think and Grow Rich*, and *Anyone Can Make a Million* were available to me. But by far the most influential book was *Save Tax in Canada and Retire at 45*. That one addressed my goal precisely, and I thought that, if I followed the advice at my young age, I had a chance of retiring at 35. It also supplied the first good lesson on taxation. All these books were written for an adult audience, and, while I didn't completely understand the investment terminology, I couldn't help but absorb the concepts. At the time, those were the only resources I had, but they formed the foundation of my plan and provided the means to learn and the advice to experiment with on my quest for financial independence.

I applied many principles of sound money management while I was still in high school and more so later in university and college. It was excellent practice to use the concepts, and I saw the results of handling income from student jobs, finding ways of getting additional income, paying my own expenses, saving money by choosing cheaper alternatives, and then investing whatever was left over.

My first job was working behind the scenes for the regional public library head office, from 4–6 p.m. after school. My brother was already working there, and I had him to thank for asking if there was an opening for me. Shortly after I was hired, however, I had the feeling that my time and effort weren't as valuable there as my brother's. Since I'd learned typing in school, the head librarian asked me to type an expense report she had written out in rough. I laboured over fitting the column headings across the top of the page and made sure all the decimal points lined up perfectly in each column. It took a long time to finish, but I proudly left it on her desk. The next afternoon, she was waiting with the report in her hands, and she didn't appear to be as pleased as I'd expected. Looking down through glasses pinched at the end of her nose, she said to me, "The column in my report for Personnel Expenses isn't done correctly. You've typed it *Personal* Expenses, and there is quite a difference between those two words!"

The second part-time job I held was in a gift shop. I greeted customers and offered them candy, created displays, and made candy trees. At Christmas time, the owner received a large order for turkey gift baskets to be made up for a local manufacturer's Christmas party. She didn't have the space or the refrigeration facilities to keep 150 frozen turkeys, so she arranged for her mother and me to arrive well before daybreak on the morning of the company's party. The truckload of turkeys was already there, and the three of us frantically passed the frozen birds around, added more food to the baskets, quickly wrapped them, and heaved them back on the truck for delivery. The Christmas rush in retail provided good experience, but shortly after the frozen turkey escapade the owner's niece arrived on the scene. I showed her the job duties as instructed and watched my work hours decrease. Then I was welcomed into the "real world" and completely squeezed out of my job.

That was another financial learning experience. Even though I had provided the desired value for the employer's money, other factors had come into play to hinder my income-generating activities. Life wasn't fair. Nevertheless, I knew that if I wanted financial freedom I needed money to pay for it. I was also learning that I had far less control over incoming money than I did over outgoing money. I didn't earn much from these first two jobs, but I followed my mother's rule of saving at least half. As long as I felt that my goal was more important than the multitude of wants that kept springing up, it was easy to save even more. Although the experiences from these two jobs weren't positive, they did supply additional motivation for my goal of not having to work.

My brother was two years ahead of me in school, and he was able to save for a good portion of his university costs from his after-school jobs and summer employment. One summer he drove a diaper-service truck, but his most lucrative work was at a canning factory. I had worked for my parents in their real estate office for a time, and the experience was invaluable. My typing had also improved immensely by then, but postsecondary school costs required summer work like my brother's that would pay more serious money. My parents asked all their acquaintances if there were any "unadvertised" student openings at their workplaces. As a result, one friend of the family graciously helped me to find a job with Bell Canada. It was excellent full-time pay with overtime, and it added to my bank balance nicely. Then, in turn, I was able to find a position for my brother at Bell when the canning factory workers went on strike and he lost that lucrative summer job. Quality family themes such as "We all help out" and "You've got a voice" were put to good use in such situations. Both are very important in building wealth. Help others whenever you can, and ask, ask, ask for whatever you need. Keep on asking until you get it.

The following summer, I wanted to return to Bell, but the company only had placements for students to work out of town. I tried to persuade my parents that the relatively high income justified the extra costs of living away from home. Unbelievably, they agreed, and I was on my own in Toronto! It was my first experience with handling money for grown-up expenses such as rent, food, and transportation, and I chose inexpensive alternatives in order to save as much as possible from my salary. I started out renting a room in a townhouse that a young couple owned, but I moved to a cheaper room in a single woman's house that was closer to work. The public transit system was very convenient and economical. I didn't eat in fast-food restaurants or order take-out. Instead, I had a full meal at lunch in the staff cafeteria and bought groceries at a nearby supermarket to make simple, light breakfasts and suppers.

One Saturday when I was at the plaza for groceries, I noticed a store called Bargain Harold's. I had never been in a discount store before. My worldly goods had come from a high-quality department store, and I'd kept each item as long as possible by fixing it or making alterations, and my remaining possessions were homemade. I was curious about the low-price store but hesitant to go inside, imagining the "kind" of people who shopped there. Finally, after thinking I wouldn't likely see anyone I knew, I ventured in. There was a jumble of what my grandmother would have called "junk and garbage," mostly poor-quality clothes and home textiles. However, there was a perfectly fine blouse in one of the bins, and I bought it for a ridiculously low price. And I found some grocery items on my list that were priced lower than what I was about to pay next door at the supermarket. I'd stumbled across a way to greater savings by choosing alternatives. Although I didn't tell anyone I was a discount shopper, each monetary reward helped me to cast off the "snob shop" habit. Added together, all these small savings meant that I could go out with my friends on weekends and still have a hefty amount of cash by September.

But my carefully planned summer abruptly changed one night at Ontario Place. On that perfect summer evening, the Bell summer students got together at an open-air café with a tented dance floor. The warm night and energetic disco moves made thirsty people, so I shouldn't have been surprised at the intoxicated state of almost everyone there. Except me, of course. Harmless fun was about to change into my first experience with disability insurance. The disk jockey had chosen a lively polka, and some clod I'd never met before pulled me onto the dance floor to show me his moves. 'Polka boy' had a vise grip but lacked any coordination. He bandied me about, a captive rag doll in his frenzied dance. Apparently, his inebriation affected his hearing, and he was completely oblivious to my yells to unhand me. I finally managed to escape back to the table, but by then my ankle was severely injured. Later it swelled to the point where I had to cut off my sock in pieces. The doctor decided that a cast was best, which meant I was on my way back home, off work, and immobilized. Fortunately, I'd been a Bell employee long enough to qualify for disability insurance, and I received reduced payments while I was off work. Even though I was able to return to my job before the end of the summer, my total earnings were quite low. But they would have been much lower without the insurance payments.

That episode taught me the importance of planning for emergencies and disabling circumstances. It also provided another example of having more control over outgoing money than incoming money. Whether income was in the form of insurance payments or salary, though, I put my money into Canada Savings Bonds (CSBs) and trust company guaranteed investment certificates (GICs). In the summers, I used 30- to 90-day GICs. The term depended on when I received the money and when I'd need it. They were all short-term savings investments, needed within a year's time. Interest rates were highest on the CSBs and trust company GICs, as opposed to bank products, and there was an added bonus with the CSBs. You could buy them a few weeks after the November 1st start date of the bond and still get the full month's interest. Meanwhile, the money earmarked for the bond would be earning interest at another institution. Same money but double the interest income stream. Back then, savings accounts paid a decent return, and the tax treatment for interest income was much better, so it was worthwhile to take advantage of the overlap. I remember my mother regularly calling brokerage firms, banks, and trust companies to compare term deposit, GIC, treasury bill, and other government bond rates. It was a good lesson illustrating that comparison shopping was necessary for all kinds of purchases, including investments.

I returned to my job at Bell with only two weeks remaining until university started. It was a relief to have a full paycheque again, but I was looking forward to living on campus and making some progress toward my goal of early retirement. As it turned out, life in residence was also full of financial experiences. Even though I didn't have much money coming in, I was responsible for my outgoing cash flow. I had earned enough for half of all my university costs, and my parents covered the balance. When possible, I bought used books for my courses and chose the inexpensive residence food plan. Meals did get a bit boring after a while, but there was a Wednesday night all-you-can-eat spaghetti special at a local restaurant and a decadent ice-cream shop for a rare treat around the corner. While it would have been cheaper to buy treats and keep them in the residence fridge, I soon discovered that food was frequently stolen. Next lesson: if you have something in demand, someone (or something) will want to steal it. My roommate and I tried to keep apples fresh in the winter by hanging them in a plastic bag just outside our window. The squirrels stole them.

But there were also positive money experiences. I took

advantage of many free opportunities offered by the university. There were music-practice rooms in the residence and a homey library with a fireplace. I took part in free ballet classes and swimming at the recreation centre. Free concerts were plentiful, as were residence parties and movie nights. There were more than enough free fun activities to fill spare time.

As well, I had a television and a stereo in my room, which was unusual for a student to have at the time. Although the TV was only a black-and-white portable, it was better than no TV, which is what everyone else had. For the stereo, I bought a top-of-the-line turntable from a discount warehouse, and my father built the other components. The homemade "amplifier" box had unmatched and unlabelled switches, but it worked well. The speakers were chosen for their custom sound, and the cabinets were made of elm, hand-picked for a nice grain, then stained and urethaned with love. I still use those speakers my father made — they are forever.

It was relatively easy being careful with expenses at university. It was a good preview of my early retirement plan in that all the basics were paid for, and I took advantage of free activities for entertainment. My student days were full and didn't leave much time for other recreation, like shopping. The residence was right in the core of downtown Toronto, near the exclusive Yorkville shopping district. I would walk by the shops, but the prices in the windows would keep me out on the sidewalk. The only time I went in was when an antique show and sale was held in an expensive store's concourse level. When I was younger, my family used to go to auctions regularly, and I developed an interest in collecting antiques. At this elite sale, though, I decided I would buy something small for myself because I had some birthday money to spend. It turned out to be the windiest day of the year. People clutched at mailboxes, newspaper boxes, and light standards to keep themselves grounded as they groped along. So the exclusive store was a refuge from the weather as well. As I toured the aisles, I quickly realized there weren't many antiques I could afford, but I really liked an emerald green miniature oil lamp. I think the vendor took pity on me as I tried to fish every last penny out of my purse for it. He accepted what I had, perhaps being compensated with the knowledge that his lamp would be treasured. I held on tightly to my purchase, contemplating the staggering winds outside, when I heard yelling behind me: "Stop! Stop!" — I turned around to see a skinny young man running through the front doors. Two security guards ran after him while everyone else watched. It was almost slapstick, the thief fruitlessly running against the wind, which reduced him to slow motion. He turned his horrified face to us as he realized his dilemma. But the two security men were also running in slow motion, now hatless with their hair plastered against their foreheads. They were strong, though, and probably eventually gained on the thief. All I saw was their struggle against the windstorm as they turned down an alley and out of view. It was a familiar lesson: if you have something of value, someone will want it. It was also yet another example of taking a financial risk, as in my childhood episode of canvassing for "charity."

I found only one opportunity for earning money at university. I had taken voice training for years, so I used one of the music rooms and taught singing, which provided a little spare cash. Very few students in my residence worked at part-time jobs. It came as a complete surprise to me when a number of young women openly admitted they were at university only to meet their future husbands. The remaining few were truly interested in their chosen fields and future careers. I was there for neither husband nor career. My goals were completely different from those of everyone else and, as such, unconventional. I reasoned that, if I had a Bachelor of Commerce degree, I could earn a substantial income that would pay for a house and assets and then retire early to pursue an artistic lifestyle. I really tried to do well, but I lacked enthusiasm for the theoretical courses, and it showed in my marks. I barely passed and knew I wouldn't be returning to university the next year.

My parents were disappointed, and I was devastated. My plan wasn't working, and I felt like a failure. But at least I didn't have to be an actuary! So now what? I decided on a new plan, slightly different from the first. My father strongly suggested I attend college, where I could still get an accounting degree. It would be a more practical course, and I could use some university credits. In my eyes, it would lead to a way of earning enough money to achieve my goal, although it would take longer with a lower salary.

I chose to live at home and attend the local college to save money. I did well in the Business Administration course, but after the freedom of university classes I felt like I'd returned to high school. My goals didn't match those of the college crowd either, and the program emphasized corporate finance, when I was really only interested in personal finance. At the time, comprehensive programs in that area didn't exist. I could have received a designation to sell stocks, mutual funds, or insurance, but to me each one was just a small part of personal finance. I didn't return to college the next year either.

My parents were disappointed again. I wasn't as devastated this time, and I thought I'd gained some financial ground. I'd saved money by living at home, by not buying a car, and by not taking on any consumer debt, and I would save money by not spending it on any more university or college courses! I thought it was time to enter the working world and start making money. I believed I'd finally be making some headway financially, and I couldn't wait for those dollars to start rolling in.

Although I thought earning an income as soon as possible was the way to financial freedom, I'd learned some valuable lessons from university and college. The most beneficial courses for gaining an understanding of the financial arena were economics, accounting, and marketing. Knowledge of economic laws and conditions made investment decisions easier. Accounting fundamentals helped in developing and simplifying personal money management tools to efficiently handle income, expenses, and investments. And marketing exposed the many psychological factors in the exchange of money, which helped me to recognize and avoid the inevitable roadblocks to financial freedom.

By this time, I had also read *How I Found Freedom in an Unfree World,* by Harry Browne, a book that greatly influenced my decisions. It presented ideas on how to find freedom from imposed cultural identities, government, and treadmill living.

I agreed with the philosophy, and perhaps that book gave me the courage to follow an unconventional path.

I questioned how further postsecondary courses would aid in achieving my life goals. The courses would have provided a degree for an eventual "professional" career, but was that how I wanted to spend my days? Years? Life? Would I be able to stop nodding off in class? Could I drag myself out of bed in the mornings to a job I didn't want or like until it paid for early retirement? I was prepared to accept short-term pain to achieve my goals, but I thought that the necessary years of education and the years of work would be incapacitating. Deciding to end a university or college education was very difficult, but I made the decision with complete commitment. Now I was a working girl!

SCHOOL LESSONS

- Read personal finance books and publications.
- Be prepared for a job loss.
- Find ways to increase income and ask for it.
- Save money with lower-cost or free alternatives.
- Be prepared for disabling circumstances.
- Comparison shop between similar investments.
- Take any other option besides student debt.
- Recognize the potential loss from theft.
- Know it's easier to control expenses than income.
- Analyse and question lifestyle choices.
- Make money decisions and devise plans.
- Commit to beneficial financial changes.

CHAPTER FOUR

FIRST THINGS FIRST

My entrance into the world of work was not a smooth one. I thought my best job prospects were in Toronto, specifically at one of the handful of Bell Canada offices there. I knew Bell had a generous stock option plan for its employees, and I wanted to take advantage of any opportunity to increase my wealth through an employer. While I waited for an opening there, I stayed with an uncle and aunt, who generously accepted a minimal rent until I became more established.

For me, the fastest route to a job was through a temporary agency. Within a few days, I was employed by a large insurance company in downtown Toronto. I had a clerical accounting position that consisted mostly of adding up batches of numbers all day. The pay was very low after the agency's fees were deducted, but the job was just a stepping stone to something better, and essentially it was paying for my expenses. After a month there, I applied to a small accounting firm and was hired as a secretary. The major partner expected that I would further my accounting education and become a greater asset to the company, but that wasn't *my* plan. The earnings from this job were an improvement, though.

For extra income, I taught remedial reading to the book-keeper's young son, since I had experience from a grade 13 English course. Even so, I waited apprehensively for the call from Bell. I was still living in my relatives' home and keeping purchases to a minimum. I went with my aunt for groceries and discovered discount warehouse food shopping! My focus remained on acquiring basic assets as quickly as possible, and every bit helped in accumulating some savings during this time. I put any money left over into savings vehicles because they allowed low deposit amounts, and interest rates in 1980–81 were relatively high, making the return especially good in relation to my low cost of living and tax bracket.

Finally, I was interviewed at Bell Canada and secured a position in the collections department. I wasn't keen on that type of work, but the salary and benefits were substantially better than those at the chartered accountants' office. I also began to realize that my aunt and uncle would have preferred a higher-paying tenant, so I needed to find another place to live. I didn't really like living in Toronto, but I had a good source of income (the first step of my plan). The easiest option was to live as close to my job as possible. I didn't want to keep renting, because the next step was to secure shelter and minimize its cost while still building an asset base. Owning a home, eventually free and clear, was the only way.

On my lunch hour, I would walk around the residential area near the Bell office and take note of the properties for sale. Then, in the evening, I'd meet with a real estate agent to view the homes. I soon learned that, although I'd been saving every penny and had a substantial down payment, I couldn't obtain a mortgage for the balance. I might have been able to manage a mortgage on a home in an outlying area; but, to be honest, I felt scared when I went by bus to some of those areas. A reassessment of my position was in order.

It was the spring of 1981, and I had just turned 21. I didn't like the high cost of living in Toronto. I didn't like working in collections. I didn't have any debts, I had savings of about $13,000, but I couldn't buy a home in an area where I felt safe. I was becoming frustrated and discouraged. Was nothing ever going to work out? Was I never going to reach my goals? The plan had seemed so simple, but it wasn't coming together. Stymied, I decided to take an extended vacation to regain perspective.

I quit my job at Bell and moved my belongings back to my parents' house. I flew to a horse ranch in Missouri, then stayed in Oklahoma, then went on to Texas. After spending those months in the States, my disappointment vanished, and my optimism returned. I concluded that financial achievement required flexibility and time. Just because my plan wasn't unfolding in the way I'd expected didn't mean it would never happen. I only had to make some adjustments.

The first two strategic steps of generating income and then buying the basics were sound. I was living at my parents' home in Hamilton that fall and took a job within walking distance at a dental lab. I assumed that making dentures wouldn't be as stressful as collections. It was a relaxed atmosphere, somewhat artistic, but so many hours of close work strained my eyes, and objects at a distance became blurry. The salary was exceptionally low as well, hindering my ability to amass savings. To supplement my income, I sold Avon door to door in my neighbourhood. One blustery winter evening, a young woman invited me into her home to display my wares. I was shivering, and my nose was running, detracting from the perfect Avon Lady image. Her husband wandered into the living room, and I introduced myself. He shook my frozen hand, looked out the window at the swirling snow, and said to me, "You've got guts, Dianne." I might have had "guts," but I didn't make a sale.

My mother likes to say that "The good are rewarded," and a former schoolteacher was fond of reciting that "Patience is a virtue," but I don't give credence to either. I was approaching my 22nd birthday, and I still didn't own a home. It was time to focus harder on finding a good source of income. Fortunately, a job became available with the provincial government. Unfortunately, it was in collections. The starting salary was mediocre at about $16,000 a year, but the benefits package and job security couldn't have been better, considering my previous job experiences. The determining factor, though, was that I would be able to buy a home within a couple of years. Could I stand collections again? I convinced myself I could. This type of job, after all, was the key to my future of financial independence. Wealth from collecting taxes. The irony of that was still to come.

I think every employee is enthusiastic at the beginning of a new job, and I plunged in, even happier on paydays. I joined the payroll savings plan for Canada Savings Bonds as a painless way to save. I moved into a tiny apartment on the 26th floor of an upscale highrise, again within walking distance to work. I probably should have weighed the new expense of rent against board at home plus transportation costs. I knew I wanted to buy a home as soon as possible, but I didn't think it would happen that year, either way. I also felt "entitled" to an apartment as compensation for working, and I didn't want the responsibilities or costs involved in buying a car. From the marketing course at college, I should have recognized the folly of rewards and entitlements used by advertisers to establish consumer buying patterns. Fortunately, my existing money-handling habits offset the potentially damaging consumer behaviour. I wasn't perfect; occasionally, I succumbed to sub-liminal messages and other marketing ploys, but I had been following a sound financial path for some time, and it had become automatic and effectively blocked the lure of adver-tising. I also believe that some rewards are needed to keep the motivation and momentum going to achieve any goal — the key factor being moderation. Occasional rewards. Quality over quantity. Apportioning limited resources (time, effort, income) to cover needs, goals, and a few wants. Unknowingly, I had kept a balanced approach in handling money with respect to my future goal, my current survival, and the all too human desire for unlimited wants. In July 1982, my net worth was about $20,000, which included Canada Savings Bonds, gold bullion, silver, and antiques. By October of that year, I could almost afford to buy a condominium!

Since my rejuvenation in the United States, I had replen-ished my savings to about $11,000. I reserved this amount for a down payment on a home and lawyer's fees. Since the bonds returned 19% interest, I decided to keep $1,000 aside for an emergency fund. My father owned a real estate company in 1982, and he had a special interest in helping his new "purchaser" to find the best home. I decided on a three-bedroom condo, built in a desirable area, with a ravine view. The unit had been owned by a busy single mother, and it needed a few repairs and redecorating. The sale price was $42,000, and I used $10,000 for a down payment. At that time, Canada Mortgage and Housing Corporation had a first-time home buyers' program in which I qualified for a $3,000 grant. I assumed the existing mortgage of $12,000 at 9.5% interest, and the vendor agreed to take back a second mortgage of $8,000 at 12% interest. The remaining $9,000 was a third mortgage obtained from my parents, interest free for a term of five years, to be paid monthly. The total mortgage debt was about 45% of my disposable income. Before I made my offer, my father calculated the three payments, taxes, and maintenance fees; the total cost for housing came to 63%, and he asked me if I could afford it. I'd been making personal balance sheets to watch my assets grow since 1980, but I'd recorded my income and expenses only in a notebook. Using those figures, I estimated that it would be possible to cover basic expenses with my remaining net earnings of $370 a month. Since my parents held the third mortgage, I knew they wouldn't foreclose if unforeseen circumstances forced me to miss a payment, and there was enough in my emergency fund to cover two or three months of total mortgage costs. Without their help, though, I wouldn't have been able to get such an early start in the real estate market.

At 22, I was a homeowner! So far, I had been following my plan, learning from experiences, making the necessary changes, trying again, and muddling through. Combined with new household, daily living, and renovation costs, the mortgages were a sobering challenge, but achieving every small step in my plan was exhilarating. I would go from room to room, marvelling that the whole condo was mine! It was large, and the big rooms diminished what little furniture I had. The living room suite was my parents' well-kept 25-year-old sectional sofa and chair, which my father reupholstered 17 years earlier. The end tables and window sheers were handed down in perfect condition from other relatives. I bought a marked-down brass headboard from the Sears Clearance Centre for the guest room and rescued a 1900s dresser with an oval mirror destined for the city dump. It only needed a coat of glossy white paint. When I mentioned to my mother that I needed to buy more furniture and drapes, she exclaimed, "Buy? *Buy?* You can sew drapes yourself! As for the furniture, we'll see what we can do." All my mother's side of the family exude great confidence, and they've done quite well financially. I recall that one of the few English words they regularly spoke with emphasis was "Sure!" as in "Sure I (you) can do it!" immediately followed by a rhetorical "Why not?" My father's side had gentler, more practical personalities. When I suggested to my mother that I didn't have her talent for sewing drapes, Dad smiled down at the floor and quietly took a step back as Mom began her evangelistic "Sure! Why not?" speech: "Of course you can make your own drapes! You're from this family — you're one of us. You can do *anything* you set your mind to." In jest, my father snapped to attention behind her, while I pictured petite Brigadier-General Mom commanding her soldiers "Onward brave troops — *charge!*" Making drapes seemed to be an easy task after an oration like that.

I had my mother's old sewing machine, and, as I began to make the window coverings for each bedroom, I repeated to myself that they didn't need to be perfect, they just had to look good. I gleaned coping skills from a library book called *Diana Phipps's Affordable Splendor.* It was subtitled *An Ingenious Guide to Decorating Elegantly, Inexpensively, and Doing Most of it Yourself.* This designer had her decorating featured in *Architectural Digest* and *House Beautiful.* The book jacket listed royalty and a well-known author as clients. If her techniques were good enough for them, then they were good enough for me. My mother expected perfection in her sewing, but my home would have remained bare if I'd shared her viewpoint.

One room became a den. My father panelled the walls in knotty pine while I sewed cushions for comfortable seating on a borrowed deacon's bench. For the master bedroom, I made two fabric hanging lamps from a kit, each one coordinating with the Dresden plate quilt my mother had sewn for the bed. I inherited a suite of two walnut dressers and bed from my grandparents. Round bedside tables were made from inexpensive plywood and covered with homemade matching tablecloths and square lace toppers cut from a piece of old curtain and dyed to match. The ensuite bathroom had white fixtures and walls decorated with a delicate blue-and-white paper. I simply added a wall-to-wall piece of white fake fur, which cost about five dollars at a textile outlet, for the feel of luxury beneath my feet.

The kitchen needed the most attention. It had an old linoleum floor and dated, dark green, imitation wood cabinets. I picked out a discounted end piece of new flooring, and my father laid it for me. The countertops were an acceptable off-white arborite, but all the cupboard doors were replaced with new solid pine fronts, the wood fashionably "detailed" and finished by my father as well. The eating area consisted of two wooden farm chairs and a card table with a piece of plywood cut in a circle for the top. I made a tablecloth, matching chair cushions, and a grass-cloth hanging lamp. My mother sewed coordinating placemats.

Since the appliances weren't included in the purchase price, I had to find a refrigerator and a stove. We found a stainless steel stove that was old but free, and it worked well. For $235, I bought a used gold refrigerator advertised in a newspaper. The only other purchases were an oak dining room set for about $150, again from the Sears Clearance Centre, and a new microwave from a discount appliance store for an extravagant $600. Adding the renovation and redecorating costs into the housing expense brought the total up to 67% of monthly net income, or $670 a month.

The remaining $330 per month covered food, transportation, property insurance, personal care, clothing, households, furnishings, and gifts. There weren't any spare funds for savings, so I considered the upgrades to my home as my investment plan, which amounted to four percent of disposable income. Medical and dental expenses were paid for by my employee health plan. There was no money for entertainment, vacations, hobbies, or recreation, but to me the sacrifice was justified. I owned a home. Basic costs were covered. I had an emergency fund. I was on track for my goal. Despite this logical reinforcement, I still needed ways to ebb occasional feelings of deprivation. Lifestyle was important: if I didn't feel poor, I would stay motivated and pursue my financial objectives. I needed some balance.

To alleviate the problem of having no cash for fun activities, I used the indoor pool and tennis courts at the condo complex for free recreation. Instead of paying for classes, I read library books and magazines on my various hobbies. For entertainment, I had "bring your own" parties, visited with friends and family at their homes, and enjoyed free local events. My father found and fixed a colour TV for me, and, while my stereo was perfectly adequate, I did buy a cassette deck. I had been to Florida, Jamaica, Missouri, Oklahoma, and Texas in the past two and a half years, so I was satisfied for a while with the travelling I had done. Even so, there was more I could do to improve my quality of life for free.

By keeping costs to a minimum for items that were necessary but gave me little pleasure, and by cutting out what I considered to be automatic and unnecessary purchases, I could splurge on the things I really wanted and never feel deprived financially. There were four benefits from getting accustomed to buying very little: I avoided the expensive habit of automatic buying, my home was uncluttered, I differentiated between the things that would bring lasting pleasure and those that would bring momentary pleasure, and I saved a lot of money. I continued to save by using public transportation instead of buying a car, which for me would have been a low-pleasure purchase. Transportation was a necessity, but I paid the least possible amount for it. I had money for what I determined to be high-pleasure-generating purchases. Microwave. Oak dinette. Cassette player. Brass headboard. Fur carpet. I didn't buy these desired goods on credit, so I avoided potential money problems. I had the cash to buy them by saving money many times over through (a) cutting costs on low-pleasure-generating items, (b) choosing cheaper alternatives, (c) getting things free, and (d) not purchasing some items at all.

My income was a precious limited resource, so I spent it according to my specific priorities (goals, needs) and preferences (pleasures). It was a new turn on the principle of value for money. I saw the purpose of my fridge as simply cold storage, so I had the most value for the least money by buying it used. Almost 20 years later, that fridge is with me, and I'm still waiting for its demise. Most of my furnishings were handmade, used, or free. I wasn't buying much of anything except quality. I bought a few expensive things, paid for by not buying little ordinary things such as kitchen gadgets, magazines, decorating trinkets, housewares, and hundreds of other rarely used items of minuscule value that simply waste space. Anyone who has ever had a garage sale will know the next-to-worthless value of ordinary clutter and gadgets. What someone else will pay for rarely used or unwanted items is one determination of value. The items that I did buy had inherent value — to me and to others. Recently, I sold my dining room suite for a higher price than I paid for it 17 years earlier. I still use the microwave and cassette deck, and they have never needed repairs. Quality, not quantity. One reward, not multiple rewards. Interior designers advise having one focal point, one outstanding or oversized piece as opposed to many insignificant little furnishings. I applied that rule with one more major indulgence.

In November 1983, I bought a beautiful piece of antique jewellery. My parents had received an invitation to a national travelling show of antique jewellery. It was closed to the general public, but my mother felt justified in extending the invitation to her immediate family. It was on a Saturday evening, and long-stemmed roses were handed to each lady upon arrival. An abundant buffet of delicacies had been laid out, and uniformed older men, looking like butlers, offered champagne to the guests. The champagne was very fine, and, when my brother asked for the name of the vintner, one butler intoned haughtily, "It's Mum's, of course."

There were so many unusual heirlooms on display, including an Egyptian gold ring embossed with hieroglyphics. An enamelled gold locket, from 1870, caught my eye — and I wanted it. When I started discussing the price with the store manager, my mother looked worried, but I could feel that inherited Old Country confidence. The locket was something I really wanted, so I bought it. I was able to negotiate for a heavier, longer chain to go with it but not for a lower price. Since it was valued not only as jewellery but also as an antique, the store guaranteed to buy it back at any time for what I paid. That was another example of inherent value.

I didn't know exactly where the money for the locket would come from, but I did know I'd be sorry if I left the store without it. I just had to find the money for it. My mind was racing. Three mortgages. I wasn't spending money even for an occasional magazine. But I wouldn't feel poor with a piece of jewellery like that! The manager solved my problem by offering interest-free payments over four months. I left the first cheque and went home to figure out where the next three payments would come from.

I would have to do a more intense cash flow analysis than I did before I bought the condo. In that case, I estimated many of my expenses; however, when it became apparent that I had $370 per month to budget, allocating the money among the different expense categories made the condo purchase feasible. Now, with this unexpectedly large purchase, I had to make new calculations. During 1983, my salary was raised to $18,000 a year, increasing my disposable income by about $125 a month. Also, the renovations were finished, so that expense was eliminated, and two months before the jewellery purchase I decided to rent one of the condo rooms to a student. The additional income and the reduced total expenses would cover the price of the antique locket. Just. Perhaps I was putting myself in a precarious financial position, but I still had the $1,000 bond plus 19% accrued interest for an emergency. If I was careful, I could handle the next jewellery payments.

Unfortunately, renting out the room was not a success. Four months into the term, my student tenant left by mutual agreement following her invitation one day to the university football team to use the shower after a rainy game. When I came home from work that day, I stepped in wads of mud on the broadloom and found filthy wet towels strewn throughout my home. The student wasn't there, and I decided I liked it better that way.

But that made the money situation very tight for the last two jewellery instalments. I paid the mortgages, kept the savings bond intact, and ate wherever I was invited. With transportation a fixed expense, the only adjustment I could make was to the food category. I didn't need money for any other area since I'd already learned to stockpile bargain-priced staples, and I had enough in supplies to last a few months. Cutting food costs was difficult but not impossible, and my nutrition actually improved when I eliminated expensive convenience foods. I took my lunch to work every day, and I didn't buy snacks at the coffee cart. I bought enough groceries for two months of breakfasts and lunches, and the money left over paid for slightly more than a month of suppers. I ate chili on weekdays for a month, dined out with my boyfriend on Saturday evenings, and visited my family on Sundays for dinner. It sounds like poverty living, but I saw it as a challenge, and it was only for two months. My mother suggested I delay their mortgage payment, but I decided not to. This was a test for me. If I could survive a difficult money situation now, surely I could handle any future problems. Then, just as I was really getting tired of eating chili, I had some good fortune.

One night while I was reading the area's free newspaper, I saw a cartoon game in which two drawings looked identical but in fact had some obscure differences. The skill was in finding as many of those differences as possible. For fun, I started solving the puzzle and then realized it was an entry for a contest. A new Kentucky Fried Chicken restaurant was opening nearby, and in celebration it was holding this contest. The winner would receive a huge barrel of chicken! I could almost taste it. Could that contest have been heaven sent? All I knew was that I needed to win it. I listed every discrepancy I could find, even those likely to have been print irregularities. In the end, I found over 25 differences and mailed in my list. Maybe the good really are rewarded. I won the barrel of chicken.

Although the two months were financially restrictive, I was motivated to follow through by knowing that they were a temporary pain for a pleasurable gain. I trusted my ability to control money and reaped the reward: I was healthy, happy, and had a new treasure.

Meanwhile, many changes were taking place at the tax office. A number of older employees were reclassified or offered early retirement packages, or their positions simply became redundant, allowing a flood of young people with university degrees into newly created positions. It was another example of having far less control over incoming money than outgoing money. I had thought unionized government jobs were completely secure. At the same time, my supervisor encouraged me to take a degree course in credit management. He indicated that a promotion would likely follow, along with a move to the head office in Oshawa. I signed up for the course, seeing the change of residence as a temporary concession that would further my goal of building assets through a higher income.

Shortly into the course, though, I realized that the shine on my job was quickly losing its lustre, and I wasn't enjoying studying similar material at home. So one night I sat down with my calculator and compared the pros and cons of the additional education. My job was only a means to an end, not a career. It was a necessary evil to be endured for as short a time as possible. If I didn't pass the course, I wouldn't be compensated for the tuition. I was able to move to Oshawa, but I didn't want to. My income would be higher, but so would my cost of living. Then I came up with the figures that decided my path. After I did calculations on a tax form both before and after the raise, I discovered that the increase in my disposable income would be negligible. Then, when I considered the additional costs I would incur, along with the effects on my personal goals and enjoyment of life, I decided that the designation and the promotion would be a hindrance, not a help.

When the first course on credit counselling was over, so was my participation in the program. That was my first important lesson in taxation. It was ironic that my wealth (after increased work-related costs) would have remained almost the same while the government would have reaped more from me in taxes since I would have moved into a higher tax bracket. My extra time and effort would have improved the government's coffers better than mine. In all my financial transactions from then on, I checked the numbers and did the math before making any decisions.

By March 1984, I had been living in my condo for over a year. Although the spacious interior had been upgraded and all the windows had a treetop view of the ravine, I was finding the long bus ride to work tedious. I still didn't want a car, so I considered moving closer to downtown. I hadn't been able to buy an apartment near work before, but real estate was taking an interesting turn. My father provided me with a cur-

rent market evaluation of my home, and I was pleasantly surprised at the increase. It was the beginning of an inflationary
real estate market and what proved to be my ticket to a more
convenient condo.

I was serious about moving, but as a trial I listed the condo
for $59,900. There was an immediate response, and it rapidly
sold for $58,000. I had paid the mortgages down by about
$2,000, leaving a total still owing of $27,000 to be discharged
with the proceeds. That left $31,000. My father waived his real
estate commission, saving me about $1,700, and once the other
realtor's and lawyer's fees were paid I had $29,000 in cash.

The condo's value had risen by 38% in a year and a half.
However, the return on my $10,540 investment (down payment
plus renovation costs) was 155%, calculated as follows:

Proceeds from sale:	$29,000
Less down payment plus costs:	(10,540)
Balance:	$18,460
Less difference in 15 months of payments if I had rented:	(2,115)
Total profit:	**$16,345**

The increase in sales activity and resale value seemed so extreme
that I thought prices would stagnate for a while. I was almost
24 and knew I wanted to live downtown. I had three months
until the closing date, and I chose to move back to the upscale
apartment building where I was a tenant prior to buying my
condo. I would think about my next move there.

Since I assumed real estate values couldn't possibly keep increasing to the extent they already had, I thought the best financial course of action was to rent and invest my proceeds for a superior return. I also expected to save a greater portion of my income since the monthly rent of $488 was much lower than the mortgage payments, property taxes, and maintenance fees of $629. As a percentage of net income, my rental housing costs would be about 40%. Therefore, I reasoned, I could amass an even greater down payment for the next property and continue to indulge in a few big luxuries, ignoring any small ones, as I did before.

My expenses for 1984 and 1985 averaged about $900 a month. I had recorded a bank survey showing the average person's spending habits, and the total monthly expenses came to $1,035. The biggest difference was that my cost of living, not including housing, was 33% of total expenses, while the average person spent 67%. Even as a tenant, my spending habits were opposite the average of one-third housing and two-thirds living costs. Even though my disposable income had risen and my shelter costs had declined, I was keeping other expenses to 33% of total expenditures, just as I did in the previous two years. I was able, therefore, to use the extra money for savings. According to that bank study, the average person saved less than five percent of disposable income, whereas I saved about 25% in 1984. Those figures reinforced belief in my ability to build capital, but I was about to learn a good lesson in predicting future economic conditions.

Using historical data that showed the degree of increases in housing prices over time, I concluded that the recent rise in real estate values had created an overvalued market and that prices in the near future might decline. So I thought that I should rent for a while and keep track of downtown real estate values. By the fall of 1985, I had a net worth of about $55,000. I was enjoying luxuries and accumulating money, but my numbers weren't coinciding with the current market data. Although my assets were growing as planned, real estate prices continued to escalate. I quickly decided to look for another condo, this time closer to my workplace. My father suggested two luxury buildings in the downtown core. The first building had one- and two-bedroom apartments, mostly owned by others my age. The second building had two- and three-bedroom apartments with a much older clientele. I preferred the first location, and I made my best offer on a one-bedroom unit with a storage room. The vendor didn't accept my offer, but it was all I could afford.

My second choice was a two-bedroom unit in the other complex. This time, my offer of $74,000 was accepted. I decided on $30,000 for the down payment and kept $10,000 aside for an emergency fund, renovations, savings, and cash. The mortgage payment at $424 per month was less than the rent I was paying. I chose a smaller down payment because there were still taxes and monthly maintenance fees to consider. My job was also becoming more of a strain, and I thought I might need the cash in case I quit. Even so, the down payment was a hefty 40%, and, since I didn't have any other consumer debt, I was able to obtain a mortgage for the remaining $44,000 easily.

I had never applied for a bank mortgage before, but after

comparison shopping for rates I decided on a major trust company. I made an appointment, and I was a little nervous, not knowing what to expect. The loans officer sat behind a huge mahogany desk, and I felt dwarfed in my chair. She was looking over the agreement of purchase and sale, the mortgage application, and my proof of income. Then she pulled out a list and started asking questions about my financial position.

"Do you have any other outstanding debts?"

"No."

She eyed me and asked me more specifically, "A car loan?"

"No."

"Are you making instalment payments for anything?"

"No."

"Any other mortgages?"

"No."

"Are you carrying a balance on your credit card?"

"No."

"Have you ever declared bankruptcy?"

"No."

"Well, that was easy," she said.

It took less than ten minutes to approve the mortgage. Since I was so security conscious, though, I opted for a 25-year amortization, which had the lowest monthly payment. The mortgage contract also allowed for monthly "double up" payments and a 10% repayment on the anniversary date. Those payments were applied directly to reduce the outstanding principal on the loan. By now, after years of practice, my money-handling skills were efficient and cost effective. I could safely handle the monthly mortgage amount even with unexpected financial problems, and if everything stayed the same I would be able to take advantage of the double-up payments and the yearly 10% reduction, instead of depositing the money into savings vehicles as I did before. I was covering all eventualities. In the worst case, I wouldn't likely lose my condo or equity. In the best circumstances, I would eliminate my debt as if I had taken a much shorter amortization simply by making extra payments *at the beginning* of the mortgage, effectively lowering the principal faster and in turn the total interest paid. I had my mortgage, and the process had been painless.

The complete housing cost of $693 now represented about 50% of my disposable income, which increased to $1,400 per month in 1986. This cost for shelter was only $64 a month more than what I was paying for my first condo four years earlier, yet it represented 67% of total *expenditures* for 1986. All other expenses remained at 33%. As a percentage of new disposable *income*, however, other costs of living amounted to 20%, and the remaining 30% became savings, which included mortgage-reduction payments. It had become an unconscious habit to keep my costs of living to about one-third of total expenses, regardless of any increase in disposable income. When I received a raise in income, it automatically became savings, simply because I maintained my expenses at the same level as before. I didn't budget a set percentage ahead of time, but I'd focused on monthly expenses for years, and I'd become very efficient at keeping the costs down without feeling deprived. Even as a tenant, my living costs (without rent) remained at the same level: 33% of all expenses.

While setting limits on budget categories never worked for

me, knowing my goals and spending priorities did work. After I put savings toward paying down the mortgage, the rest was for RRSP contributions and luxuries. Transportation costs were almost nonexistent because I was still within walking distance to work and shopping. An underground parking spot came with my unit, but since I didn't have a car I was able to rent the space for $20 a month. The other budget categories were relatively low because I didn't need to look beyond my home environment for recreational activities.

The condo building's indoor pool and Jacuzzi opened onto a patio with lounge chairs and umbrella tables, all enclosed by a high brick wall. There was an exercise room full of equipment and a library for less strenuous pursuits. Since the building was filled with older residents, they would be in their units by 9:30 p.m., which meant I had the pool and other facilities virtually to myself in the evenings. A penthouse party room contained plush furniture, a kitchenette, and a bar for entertaining. My own unit had central air conditioning, an ensuite laundry area, and an enclosed balcony that I made into a tropical sunroom. I sewed white sheers for the large window; then I laid green outdoor carpet on top of a scrap piece of broadloom for underpadding, and I applied white stucco to the concrete wall. I painted my wrought iron sewing machine cabinet white and placed it against one glass wall. The seating area contained two rattan chairs, which I bought at a garage sale, placed around a table constructed of a milk can for its base, a plywood circle for its top, and a colourful Caribbean-print sheet for a full-length tablecloth. A large white glass ball lamp, another garage sale find, hung over the table.

Then I filled the room with exotic plants, most of which I had started from cuttings.

Again I was paying the least or nothing at all for items of low value whenever possible. I had all the same furniture as before except for the living room suite. I bought a tweed sofa and a leather sofa bed, both in taupe tones. Small accessories and soft furnishings were inexpensive to change, so I followed the interior design rule of buying the most durable and expensive furniture in neutral colours. I also bought a floor-model wing chair, priced to clear, and a coffee table with two end tables on sale. I made these purchases over three years, only after I had saved enough money first. That way I knew exactly what they cost, and I could accurately judge their value in exchange for my money or, stated another way, for the time and effort given up to make the net income. If I'd charged the furniture on my credit card and then carried a balance, it's staggering to think what the true purchase prices would have been. And, regardless of the additional interest costs, I wouldn't have been controlling my money. The store or finance company would have had control over my present *and* future dollars. It was far better for the asset value (cost of the item) and other asset accumulation (savings) to simply wait for a few months, buy exactly what I wanted for cash, and then use the money I would have lost (interest charges) to buy the next pleasure-generating item. That was controlling my money.

My aversion to debt was reinforced by working in a field that brought me face to face with people in dire straits. I saw firsthand what happened to people who couldn't meet their financial obligations. When their income didn't cover expenses, they borrowed money (illegally in the case of Sales Tax) month after month and then became grossly overextended. My job duties included instigating wage garnishments, seizing assets and bank accounts, and registering liens. It was real life and real people. I wanted to make sure I would never be on the receiving end of such actions.

While it was a difficult part of my job to see the consequences of the desperate financial moves people made, it was interesting to see the results of the money decisions made by those in my workplace. In the 1980s, conspicuous consumption was in high gear. I wasn't immune to it, and I bought my share of luxury goods while I was renting. Psychologically, I took the set mortgage payments more seriously, even though I could expect a yearly increase in my rent, which effectively lowered my disposable income. However, I still maintained my principles of buying with cash, acquiring goods that had inherent value, and only making purchases that gave me the greatest satisfaction. My idea of indulgences, though, didn't match average consumption trends. I didn't use credit to buy a popular car or pay for regular winter and summer vacations. I didn't buy everyday lifestyle products as others automatically did, even if the products were inexpensive. But I did buy a large wardrobe, jewellery, and a fur coat. Although no one believed me, I really did want the fur for warmth. It was so cold walking to work in the winter, and I refused to wear a down-filled coat and look like a huge quilted pillow tottering down the street.

As for vacations, ever since I'd been to Jamaica, I didn't understand the attraction my fellow employees had for going en masse to inexpensive hot destinations such as Cuba, the

Dominican Republic, and Mexico. I still don't. To me, frequent jaunts to popular places offer short-lived satisfaction, whereas infrequent luxury vacations provide greater happiness. It's simply a matter of personal choice. The most economical holiday is the one that provides the best value in terms of lasting pleasure. My brother and sister-in-law travel to Mexico frequently because it's their favourite vacation spot, so it's the best financial choice for them. Likewise, when I had the chance to meet a friend in France during the summer of 1987, I took it. I arranged for time off work during the first three weeks of August. However, since I'd been to France before, I was concerned about the long flight from Canada and my susceptibility to travel sickness. My father jokingly said, "You could always take the Concorde." I liked the idea, so I did. The chance to travel throughout France with my friend, then on to England, where I had always wanted to visit, was too good to miss. The total cost for my trip, including the airfare on the Concorde, was the same as three vacations to Mexico. I wouldn't have traded that trip for six trips to Mexico.

I flew first class from Toronto to La Guardia airport and then continued on in a waiting limousine to JFK airport. Air France covered the cost. Once at JFK, I was cordially greeted at the door. My suitcase was whisked away, and my hand luggage was graciously carried for me as I was escorted to the Concorde lounge. It was like a large, plush living room, with subtle lighting and a long bar at the end. Glistening silver trays of puff pastry hors d'oeuvres were set out, and the bartender waited patiently for me to select a drink. He looked amused when I asked for a cup of tea. I'd had a full breakfast in first class, but it was still morning, and tea was what I wanted. I sat down on a soft chair, noticing the expensive glossy magazines and the latest issue of Sotheby's auction catalogue on the coffee table in front of me. My tea was served with a plate of fresh croissants, flown in that morning from France. Everything was complimentary, and I was treated like a queen. The ladies' room was elegantly decorated with touches of gold and wall-to-wall glass shelves filled with French perfumes. I caught the bartender smiling again when I came out surrounded in scent.

When it was time to board the Concorde, the man who'd escorted me to the lounge accompanied me and along the way offered me a variety of world newspapers and magazines. On boarding, I was introduced to my host, who was to look after me for the duration of the flight. He had handsome French features and was young and striking in his Air France uniform and gloves. He would have looked great on the cover of the magazine I was holding. Could it get any better? It did.

The take-off was a roar of engines one second and a surprisingly inclined lift the next. It did not taxi down the runway like other planes. Once airborne, there was no turbulence at the altitude we were flying, and I couldn't even tell that the plane was in motion. Menus announcing a five-course meal were handed out to whet the appetite. Complimentary cocktails, liqueurs, wines, and champagnes were also listed. I chose Dom Ruinart, 1979. To start, I had the canapé appetizers, followed by a lobster-and-vegetable salad. The main course was medallion of lamb with Madeira and chapped truffle sauce, chanterelle mushrooms sautéed in olive oil, and potatoes gratin.

For dessert, a Grand Marnier genoese cake. As the final course, a luscious fruit salad plate was served. When the china was cleared, my host invited me to meet the pilots and view the cockpit. He suggested I bring my camera, and when I entered the tiny cabin area the pilot motioned for me to sit in the seat behind him while my French host took my picture. When I returned to my seat, the other flight attendants were busy giving out Concorde portfolio cases and toiletry bags. It had been just over three hours, and the flight was coming to an end. My host charmingly asked if there was any final thing he could do for me. I thought of all kinds of things but simply thanked him for his attentions.

The final approach to Charles de Gaulle airport was like being in an air show. The plane banked fiercely on one side and then on the other in a nose-dive. Just before landing, the back end flattened down first, and then the front, where I was seated, gently rocked forward to meet the tarmac. The engines roared in a great reverse thrust, violently shaking the insides of the plane, and like an anticlimax it simply stopped.

French Customs was a short distance from where we disembarked, and I was immediately led to a congenial official who actually smiled and waved me through. I didn't remember my last time at French Customs being like that.

I felt no ill effects from the trip over, and I was able to spend a few days in Paris, stay with friends in the French Alps, spend a week at the Riviera, travel back to Paris, then fly to London for a long weekend, all without feeling tired. For me, it's quality, not quantity, that matters. One great trip occasionally rather than three mediocre vacations regularly. At

66

STOP WORKING … START LIVING

the same time, I'd accumulated the money not spent on the ordinary trips to pay for the luxury trip, and I could enjoy myself in Europe freely.

Another spending behaviour I didn't share with my coworkers was participating in the workplace lottery pool. It just didn't seem to be proactive to me. They all hoped for a windfall of money by making weekly payments. My windfall of money would come from making regular payments to a savings plan. Over the six years I worked there, none of the lottery crowd ever came away with a pile of money, but I did. And what kind of fun was that, losing money, week in, week out, for years on end? I, not chance, controlled my money, and in the end I had a sure thing.

My spending patterns seemed to differ, in fact, in almost every area from those of my peers. One friend had a flashy new car complete with expensive lease payments, but it didn't bring her the most happiness. She wanted her own apartment, but with the hefty monthly payments on the car she couldn't afford her own place and had to keep living with her parents. And a new bride complained to me when the couple bought a run-down house. On my visits to their home, it looked like they were living in poverty, but my cousin loved shopping, and she rarely went into a store without buying something. It seemed to me that her recreational shopping was an escape as she happily went from store to store. That is, until the day I witnessed her tearful pleas while her husband locked up her credit cards. Whenever I slipped into the behaviour of buying low-value treats as rewards for enduring unsatisfactory conditions (working), I quickly corrected it by noticing the unhappy results that the habit produced in others around me.

The principles of my plan kept me from going astray as well. At the beginning of 1988, I was focusing on the time and the effort of earning money and their relative value to me, carefully examining any automatic or externally conditioned thinking patterns. I'd been doing collections since 1982, and I knew I couldn't do it much longer. My financial position was good: I had about $24,000 in my RRSP and nonregistered investments (still in gold, silver, bonds, and certificates), about $35,000 left on my mortgage, and no other debts. My net worth was now at $145,000 due to a surprising real estate evaluation that estimated my condo resale price at $140,000. However, after almost two years, even with some early repayments, I had lessened the mortgage liability by only $9,000. I knew I'd have to be more aggressive in paying it down. A retroactive pay increase in the form of a lump-sum payment was due to me at any time. The union's settlement would mean that I could look forward to an extra $9,000, which I'd apply to the mortgage.

In the meantime, my luxury condo was affordable, and it was completely furnished to my satisfaction with enough new items to keep me happy indefinitely. I had travelled to Las Vegas and Europe within the past six months, so I was content to delay travel for a while. But I would still need another job to achieve early retirement. I thought of my grandmother, who couldn't speak English well yet managed to find work throughout the Depression. She once told my mother, "You can always get a job; you can always do something." So, in the spring of 1988, just after I turned 28, I left my government job.

LAYING A SOLID FOUNDATION

- Spend consciously and determine priorities.
- Do the math before making any money decisions.
- Employers are for net income and stock option plans.
- Take advantage of moonlighting opportunities.
- Set aside an emergency fund.
- Buy a home in a good area with a 25%–40% down payment.
- Use home buyers' plans and vendor take-back mortgages.
- Stay debt free, except for a mortgage.
- Do it yourself or get it free.
- Once basic furnishings are acquired, spend disposable income as follows:

Housing	34%
All other expenses	33% (maximum)
Savings	33% (minimum)

- When disposable income goes up, keep all other expenses at the same level and add the whole increase to savings.
- Savings priorities are mortgage reduction and RRSP contributions.
- Shop at discount stores for all types of purchases.
- Buy goods with inherent value.

- Select preferred luxuries and enjoy them
  occasionally.
- Don't count on historical market data for
  forecasting.
- Jobs and spending habits must never hinder financial
  goals.

CHAPTER FIVE

ONWARD AND UPWARD

The great rush of relief after leaving such a stressful job in 1988 gave me the confidence to keep striving for early retirement. Although I needed another job, I had money saved, no debts, and a substantial increase in net worth, due mostly to the rapid rise in condominium prices. My outstanding mortgage of $35,000 on the new condo value of $140,000 amounted to only 25% debt, whereas the proportion of debt on the prior condo value of $74,000 came to 47%. The boost to my net worth provided the motivation to eliminate the remaining mortgage balance and gain the entire difference (less costs) as profit. Finding the funds to discharge the mortgage by the next anniversary date was my first priority. I had ten months.

I received a retroactive pay increase from my previous government job, and I used the money to double my mortgage payment each month. As well, my RRSP got a boost when I left work since the pension amounts deducted from my paycheques were rolled over into my existing RRSP. I asked for a pension booklet before I quit and used it to figure out the exact amount I'd receive. My figures showed that I should have received more, so I called the pension department, collect, of course. The government clerk did the calculations again and called back to confirm that my figures were right. At the end of our conversation, she asked how I'd found the error. I told her, "I just did the math."

Then, in the summer of 1988, I was offered the first fun job I'd ever had. A friend asked if I would like to work during the shows at the city convention centre and live theatre hall. She convinced me to take the job by mentioning that I'd enjoy the shows for free. There were also complimentary tickets to shows for friends and family and food to take home after various catered events. I could walk to work, and it was fun to be both behind the scenes and in the audience. The public, though, regarded the city staff as "lower life forms" and treated us accordingly. While my quality of life improved by working at a pleasurable job, it was difficult to contend with this bias, which permeated not only consumer shopping locales and types of acquisitions but also types of employment. When I chose to leave that job, the city personnel office mailed the separation certificate to me. Although I hadn't indicated why I quit, a government clerk had fabricated the reason as "personal betterment" and handwritten it on the document.

In the fall of 1988, however, I took another hard look at my financial position. A recent evaluation priced my condo at about $150,000, and the real estate market was booming. I was happy with the assets on my balance sheet, but I still wanted to be rid of my only liability, the mortgage. I determined which assets I could use for funds and analysed my expenses once again, keeping in mind the value I received for the money I spent. I'd reduced all costs except housing from 33% to about 25% of total expenditures, so I didn't think I could make any more changes there.

Next I considered housing, now at 75% compared with the other expenses. It seemed to be too expensive and out of balance for what I was receiving in return. After doing a little research, I discovered that property taxes for a house in a better area were less than what I was paying at the condo. Houses on huge lots in a nicer area were taxed $1,200 a year, whereas my condo taxes were just under $1,600. In comparing my condo with a house, I listed the following. I had only one view from my unit, and it was of another building. I didn't have a yard to enjoy. Insurance costs were about the same for either type of dwelling. Condo maintenance fees, at $175 per month, seemed to be exceptionally high versus monthly house expenses. I could gladly give up the indoor pool for the freedom of retirement. Without the government job, I didn't need to stay downtown, and I'd enjoy breathing fresher air away from the core of the city. As well, a new problem arose when a group home sprang up in the neighbourhood. I'd been approached a few times by what looked to me like "anger management" residents. But the main factor in deciding to move was that I could buy a house the same size as my condo in a desirable area on a large lot, with lower taxes, and at a lower price! I decided the condo was overvalued and ripe for selling.

Since the real estate market was so overheated, I thought I could sell my unit myself. In January 1989, I set the price at $149,900 and advertised the condo in the local newspaper. The response was encouraging, and a local real estate agent called to ask if she could bring some people to see it. We agreed that if I accepted their offer I'd pay her a selling commission of three percent but not the listing commission (an additional three percent). At the time, this was considered a normal arrangement by area realtors. After showing my home, the agent called and said the couple loved it and wanted to make an offer. I was pleased but restated our agreement about paying only the selling commission if I accepted their offer. She then said she wanted both commissions and, if I didn't agree, would simply tell the couple there was something wrong with the condo and advise them to buy elsewhere. I reminded her that wasn't the agreement, but she didn't care. Perhaps I should have made our arrangement in writing, but if that was how she conducted business before I even saw an offer I didn't want any continuing association with her. As it turned out, I made a better profit on my own. In March, I sold my home for $147,000, commission free.

By then, the mortgage anniversary date in April was less than a month away and, unfortunately, four months before the closing of the sale. I arranged for a loan of $13,000 to bridge the months to closing, used all my savings, withdrew part of my RRSP, and discharged my mortgage! I had just turned 29, and I was mortgage free.

The property value had increased by just under 100% over three years. Interestingly, the units in my previous condo complex had risen by only about 85%. Perhaps the difference was due to the real estate mantra of location, location, location.

In calculating the return on my down payment for the second condo, I considered renovation costs, advertising expenses, lawyer's fees, and the difference between housing costs if I'd remained a tenant. In total, my return on investment (original down payment + reno costs) over the three years was just under 325%, as illustrated below.

Proceeds from sale:			$147,000
Less bridge financing:			(13,128)
Total proceeds:			$133,872
Costs:	renovations	$998	
	advertising	115	
	legal fees	500	
			(1,613)
Balance:			$132,259
Less difference in housing costs			
if I had rented:			(5,160)
Balance:			$127,099
Less original investment:			(30,000)
Total return:			**$ 97,099**

It's important to note that the only time I saw my home as an investment was when I thought the price had risen too high in relation to the condo's value as housing. The primary function of a home is to provide shelter; as an asset with inherent value, though, a home has investment potential. A profit (or loss) is realized only at the time of sale, and, since I was aware of my condo's market value, I chose to capitalize on what I thought was an overvaluation within its asset class and improve my standard of living from both the profit and the intrinsic benefits of alternative housing. If I hadn't discharged the mortgage, or sold at the peak of the real estate boom, or bought another home for less money, I wouldn't have made such a good profit. I still needed shelter, and I believe it's because I treated housing as a value-rated lifestyle choice, and not as an investment, that I did so well financially.

But now I had to decide where I wanted to live next, and within a month I found a cute house near the city's university. It needed work, but that didn't deter me. My ever-practical father told me, "You can't look after a house on your own," but given my "Sure! Why not?" inheritance I was positive that I could. Besides, buying a house was a necessary step in my plan. I was getting closer to my goal all the time, acquiring basic assets for cash and building wealth along the way. This house, which cost less than the proceeds of the condo sale, would greatly improve my quality of life and allow me to live mortgage free.

My money philosophy remains as a result of my vision of a quality lifestyle: hedonism paired with gratitude. Pleasing surroundings, no money worries, enjoyable activities alone and with others, these are my priorities. Even greater happiness comes from having the time to do the things I enjoy. So I use money as an exchange of value for goods and services only after determining how much of my time and effort I must give up to get the money. Put another way, the value of any desire is determined by the amount of time and effort required to satisfy it. For example, I bought a used lawn mower to cut the grass at my house. I could have paid someone else to cut it, but it was cheaper to spend my time and effort on the grass than to hire someone else, because I would have had to work for an employer for three hours to earn the net income required to pay another person to do a 30-minute job. It was work either way: whether I cut the grass or earned the money to pay for a lawn service. Considering that my employment income was limited to 35 hours a week *maximum*, the money was better spent elsewhere. And the lawn mower was an asset with inherent value — that is, I could have sold it at some point.

My money philosophy also includes the necessity of delayed gratification and tolerable employment to produce my ideal lifestyle. Ironically, if I'd allowed instant gratification financed by debt, and pursued a profession after years of expensive education to achieve an acceptable standing, it's unlikely that I would have had the quality lifestyle by the time I reached my 40s or even 50s that I was already enjoying by age 30.

When my father realized he couldn't change my mind about buying a house, he tried to convince me to look in the most prestigious area first for one that didn't need work and take a small mortgage to cover the higher price. But that would have been a step backward in my scheme and a waste of my time. I would have needed to work many more years to pay off another mortgage. My goal now was to retire within the next four years, by the time I was 33. If I continued to work to build my RRSP and nonregistered savings, and I had a home free and clear, I would be right on schedule. I followed my money philosophy and bought that tired little house, close to the university campus, for $132,500. I moved into it in July, with a plan to take care of the most urgent repairs over the next month and rent the basement room to a student in September.

Fortunately, my father had compassion for his determined daughter, and my mother used the excuse that I didn't have a husband to help me, when they arrived with electrical supplies and mop and pail. The hazardous wiring was quickly replaced, and a shower head was added to the old three-piece bathroom. A friend helped me pull up the smelly broadloom, revealing oak flooring underneath. Then I tore off old wallpaper, patched, sanded, painted, and scrubbed the whole house.

When I moved in, the decor was gloomy. But even as I redecorated, the walls seemed to close in at night, and I couldn't sleep in the house the first month. When I finally forced myself to stay overnight, the dark house felt oppressive. Then, when the eerie noises began, I got up and opened the front and back doors, leaving only the screens locked, allowing me a hasty escape if needed. I was afraid of the inside, not the out-side, but could recognize the absurdity of this fear only in the morning — after the sun came up.

I was looking forward to a tenant for the income and for the company, because it would be easier to get some sleep if another person was in the house. My home was almost ready, and the roof was the next priority. It had just started to leak, and I didn't want to wait for ceiling damage. There was a completely finished basement already, a modernized kitchen upstairs, and scenic views of the mature treed lot from three sides. The living room had a large bay window, and I could lie on the sofa and gaze up at birds nesting in the old maple tree on the front lawn. The house was on a corner lot, 40 feet wide by 140 feet deep, with a white split-rail fence and ancient tall trees lining the perimeter. It was picturesque country living, with the conveniences of the city.

When the roof was fixed, I took applications from prospective students, but this time I was much more careful with my selection. I listened to sage advice from my parents, who were experienced with student tenants. "See if they take their shoes off when they come in," and "Choose someone who comes with their parents," they said. I used my mother's list of tenant rules and discussed it with both the potential students and their parents. Since I'd be living upstairs, we needed to have the same idea of what a good home environment would be. Many people thought it was odd that a young woman wanted to rent her basement to a male student, but I'd already had a bad experience with a female student. The one I finally chose had come with his European father and sister. I knew that many people of his father's generation had started out with boarders in their homes, and I think this family was as relieved and as comfortable as I was with the arrangement. The student turned out to be an exceptional tenant. For a small reduction in rent, he cut the grass, shovelled the snow, and took out the garbage for me. I finally slept well at night knowing that he was just downstairs.

He was so responsible that I decided to take a winter holiday in Florida. When I came back, I asked him how he'd managed. He hesitated, then said, "Fine, except it's a pretty spooky house." I thought back to those episodes of evening angst before he moved in. I waited apprehensively for him to tell me about the "happenings" he'd experienced while I'd been away, and I was relieved when we ended up laughing about them. Apparently, ever since he'd been living there, we were both attributing those strange noises in the night to each other.

By the end of 1989, I had a temporary full-time contract in a real estate office. Housing prices had peaked in the area and then stagnated into 1990. I was thankful I'd sold my condo. As long as my house expenses could be covered, the valuation didn't matter, because the house wasn't on the market (for sale), and its purpose wasn't to provide an investment return — only shelter.

Now I had to take the next steps in my plan to afford retirement in three years. My cash flow with employment and rental income was good, but I had an RRSP of less than $5,000. I'd need much more.

Since I didn't have to concentrate on mortgage costs anymore, I changed the way I recorded expenses to reflect my new focus on grouping costs in order of necessity. I wanted to channel as much income as possible into a nest egg, so I needed an easy way to review my costs of living. I ranked the remaining expenses according to necessity and categorized them based on their potential for reduction. The most necessary and unchangeable expenses represented 60% to 80% of total costs, while 20% to 40% was spent on unnecessary but fun purchases. The breakdown was much like my previous 67% for housing and savings (primary importance) and 33% for other expenses (secondary importance). I kept costs to a minimum without feeling deprived (quality over quantity). The difference between all earnings and all expenditures then accumulated as savings for my approaching financial freedom.

I'd been tracking, prioritizing, and apportioning expenses

for almost 10 years, so I felt capable of projecting total yearly expenses. Those numbers would provide an estimate of the cash flow I'd need to live comfortably in retirement. Then I could calculate the capital required in a nonregistered portfolio for the early retirement period from 33 to 65 and the amount needed in an RRSP for conventional retirement at age 65. After three years of tallying total yearly expenditures, I could determine my average cost of living per year and use that figure as a close estimate of the sum needed to finance each stage. If I had a good idea of what I'd be spending (based on what I'd been spending), then I'd have a better idea of how much I'd need. The capital in each portfolio would be supplied by the difference between net incoming cash and total outgoing expenses. Maximizing the difference to create capital was my goal. Being so close to my early retirement date provided the motivation for finding more sources of income.

I had employment earnings from both a full-time job and occasional evenings and weekend work at the convention centre. I also had rental income. And since the late 1980s, different family members had been holding garage sales periodically. While I didn't have much to sell, I could count on $75 to $200 per sale. I sold items previous tenants and homeowners had left behind, fixtures I'd replaced in renovations, unwanted donations from family and friends, and kind but unsuitable gifts I'd received. I donated a leaky dishwasher that came with the house to a charity and used the $90 receipt against my income taxes. Similarly, I donated unsold garage sale items to another charity for the tax receipts. I sold a ceiling fan and chandelier through a local "buy and sell" radio program and an old gas stove in the area newspaper's free ad section. One time, a neighbour was throwing out a wicker bookshelf that leaned to one side. I took it into my backyard, soaked it with water, and bent it straight again, weighing it down with a couple of bricks. The wicker dried in the sun, and that evening I sprayed the bookshelf white with some leftover paint. I used another free ad and sold it for $25. Individually, these means of increasing cash flow were negligible, but combined they eventually came to a sizeable sum.

By September 1990, my costs of living had amounted to only $3,600 for the previous eight months. I was happy with my cash flow, which had provided about $13,000 net income, leaving $9,400 for savings, $2,300 of which I added to my RRSP. I'd become used to my mysteriously eerie house, and I wanted to do more extensive renovations, so I decided not to have another tenant that fall. Unfortunately, general economic conditions were slowing down. My work contract covering a maternity leave was over, and I was out looking for another full-time job. Then an opportunity came along that changed the date of my financial freedom.

Although my father was working as an industrial systems specialist, he kept his real estate broker's licence and followed the local housing market. He noticed a house for sale that was a "diamond in the rough" only a few blocks from my home but in a more prestigious area. He made an appointment, and after viewing it he thought it was priced very well for a renovation project that he could work on in his spare time. My father bought it for $131,000 — less money than what I'd paid for my house six months earlier. My family went to the preclosing inspection to see his project and voice our opinions. The house did need work, but it was solid brick and stone and had a paved driveway, central air conditioning, an underground lawn sprinkler system, and a fireplace. And it was larger than my house. I wanted it.

It was a serious dilemma. I wanted to retire soon, yet I wanted to buy that house. I was practical enough to know I couldn't do both, and I was impractical enough to try. Oh, those unlimited wants! I also knew that, with my father as the vendor, it would complicate matters.

When I was growing up, my parents decided what was best for me. When I became an adult, they gradually accepted whatever I decided was best for me. They've always had a propensity to give, but they've respected my fiercely independent nature and desire to "do it myself." That being the case, I've rarely asked them for anything, but after seeing the house my resolve was shattered.

After the inspection, I invited my family over for coffee. They excitedly discussed my father's purchase, but I was unusually silent. When they all left, I waited about 20 minutes for my parents to drive home. Then I called my father and asked him, "Will you sell your house to me?"

After many long discussions, my father and I made some plans. He would renovate the house and sell it to me. I had just received a small accident insurance settlement that would partially cover the utilities, taxes, insurance, and remodelling costs while the tradesmen and my father worked on the house. The balance would be paid from my savings for early retirement and from proceeds from the sale of my existing house.

Any decorating and outside upgrades would be left up to me to finish and pay for. My retirement would have to be delayed.

In early 1991, I started working for another real estate company. It was a small business where I ran the office while the broker concentrated on sales. Although I wasn't an agent, I kept up to date on the real estate market by being immersed in listings and deals on a daily basis. Generally, the market was not doing well.

But my personal finances were improving. Total expenses at the end of 1990 were only $5,500, and at the end of 1991 they were $8,600. Considering my net income for that year was $20,100, I had about $11,500 left over: $1,700 allowable for my RRSP and $9,800 for my nonregistered savings.

I had a great deal of financial responsibility in my job. I regularly handled banking, accounts payable and receivable, rent collection, and bookkeeping. Although my boss knew I was completely capable of those duties, due to the poor market conditions at the time, he would often ask me, "How are we doing? Are there any deals coming in? Are we going to be okay?" My concern, naturally, was that he could meet payroll (it was never a problem), but he wanted to know the business's daily cash position. Since I knew the average monthly office expenses and had records of pending sales, I devised cash flow statements that detailed money coming in and going out in chronological order for 90 days in advance. At any time, he could see the company's cash flow position. The office's bookkeeping wasn't computerized, so I manually had to make adjustments for changes and make completely new statements frequently. But these statements served their purpose: he didn't want computer graphics, he wanted information. As I became adept at creating cash flow projections for the small business, I decided to do the same for my home finances to forecast my personal cash flow. That way, I could invest regularly by knowing when and how much cash was coming in, when and how much was required for expenses, and when and how much would be available for savings. I would be controlling my money efficiently, like a well-run business.

In 1992, I contributed $4,000 to my RRSP, and I had expenses of $7,800 for the year, which left $12,000 for early retirement savings. My cash situation was good. My housing circumstances were not. The renovations were nearly completed, and my house was up for sale, but I hadn't received any offers. Values were plummeting. From 1992 to 1995, I stopped recording net worth statements because I was so discouraged over the decline due to real estate prices. I wondered if my house was ever going to sell. Even though I didn't consider my home to be an investment, it was hard to watch the value go down. Other house values were decreasing relatively, but I would be suffering a loss simply because I had to sell, and the sale price after costs would be less than what I'd originally paid for the house. It was disheartening when I finally sold my home in the spring of 1993 for $127,000.

Still, it would have been much worse if I'd had a mortgage and watched it become a far greater proportion of debt as the value of the property decreased. I saw many homes come through the real estate office under forced "power of sale," where homeowners lost all their equity, and some properties even had debts exceeding their new market values. As well, considering I'd started with a $10,000 down payment and 10 years later had $122,700 cash (after costs) for housing, I had nothing to complain about. Also, if I hadn't owned a home during that time, it's doubtful I would have accumulated the same amount from the savings in rent versus mortgage, maintenance, and taxes. While I viewed housing in my plan as a basic cost-of-living expense that had to be reduced to as little as possible, my father always stressed that owning a home is a forced savings plan. It is much more difficult to access equity in a home than savings in investments, and monthly mortgage payments are much more likely to be adhered to than a savings plan. I'm sure that I would have made regular savings, but it's unlikely that I would have deposited or invested anywhere near the amount I'd paid monthly for shelter. And I don't think I would have accumulated nearly as much after 10 years.

By the time I turned 33, I'd reached my early retirement target date, but I was still working. I had a much nicer house, but it put financial freedom ahead a few years. As did the car I bought that spring.

For a couple of years after I moved into my first house, I thought about buying some kind of vehicle. That house was farther from public transportation and shopping than my condo was, and I didn't like the taxi experience. As well, getting all the supplies for the renovations from the store to my home was difficult. A car or truck was becoming more of a need than a want.

I referred to the book *Save Tax in Canada and Retire at 45* for inspiration and guidance. I'd already weighed the alternatives to owning a car and made the decision to buy one. The book suggested shopping for a bargain and buying an economical car. I only needed it for inconvenient trips (groceries and building supplies for the next house), and I didn't want to handle any mechanical problems that might arise. I decided to buy a cheap new car.

I began my research at the public library, looking at books that showed car reliability, repair and recall history, safety records, and general recommendations. I made a short list of the inexpensive models. Then I set about test-driving the list of cars. I explained to the salespeople that I didn't like driving and wanted to drive the cars in a familiar area. New car sales were not doing well in January 1993, so I found the dealerships very accommodating. Since I didn't already have a car to drive to the sales lots, I had the sales reps bring one to my workplace as I was finishing for the day. I asked them to take me to my home neighbourhood, where I changed seats for the test drive, which I finished in front of my house. Each rep looked a little surprised when I got out and said, "Thank you. I have a few more to try yet, so I'll let you know." But it wasn't that I'd just arranged a free ride home. I really did buy one of those cars.

It was a '93 Dodge Shadow hatchback with an automatic transmission, an upgraded engine, air conditioning, and a three-year, bumper-to-bumper warranty. It was larger than a similar Toyota model, and it suited my needs perfectly. After all the costs and taxes, I paid $12,000 cash for it, and the dealer delivered it to my home.

With the hatchback trunk and back seat pushed down, I

was able to move half my household belongings to the new house over a number of short trips, which saved on eventual moving costs. I could now buy food staples in bulk, also saving money that way. And I didn't take the car to work, so I saved on insurance. But it was still an expense that prolonged my working life.

Now I planned to retire within the next two years, by the time I was 35. At the end of 1993, my net income was $19,500, of which $3,900 went into my RRSP at the beginning of the year, based on my own calculations on my earnings in 1992. Expenses for the year were $8,000, not including the purchase of the car, leaving a balance of $7,600 for savings.

My cost of living was low in 1991 and virtually the same in 1992 and 1993, so I estimated expenses to continue at about $8,000 per year. (In five years of retirement, the actual figures have been in the $7,000 to $9,000 range.) Of a gross average income of $20,000 per year, my retirement income needs were about 40%, not the general "expert" financial planners' advice of 60%–80%. The amount in my nonregistered portfolio would have to supply $8,000 a year in current dollars for the 30 years until I reached 65. Since my RRSP would provide income after that, the early retirement amount could be used up by the time I reached conventional retirement age. Payments before age 65 would be made up of a portion of the accumulated capital as well as returns (gains) made on that portfolio. In retirement, my level of consumption would be only for daily living and not for any substantial acquisition of consumer goods since I already owned all the major lifestyle goods I wanted. My spending habits still reflected needs versus wants, make it or do it myself, get it free, pay the least amount, and pay cash, so the consumer price index would have little effect on me. If I wasn't buying much, then increasing product prices wouldn't matter much. Even so, I used a financial planning and insurance industry guideline to determine the amount needed: my annual income needs multiplied by a factor of 10, equalling $80,000 for my nonregistered portfolio.

To calculate the amount that I'd need in my RRSP at age 35, I used a bank's financial planning worksheet that assumed the current Canada Pension Plan (CPP) benefits would be in place and that the return on my RRSP would outpace inflation by four percent. By the time I reached retirement age, CPP benefits of some sort would be likely since I'd be considered a low-income Canadian. I allowed for a higher retirement income of $15,000 yearly, as expressed in present dollars, and I would not make another contribution to the RRSP. The calculations showed that at 35 I'd require $20,000 in my RRSP.

I knew the amount was only an estimate, since future rates of return, inflation, and income requirements can't be known with any degree of certainty ahead of time. But if this amount turned out to be grossly deficient, I still had many options to avoid any future financial constraints. I didn't need to live in such an expensive area or even within the city. I had a range of assets that could be converted to cash. I'd be young enough to work full time, if needed, during the next 30 years. I also expected to receive some part-time earnings from employment or my own business in the future, but they'd come from a fun job of my own choosing or from a hobby. That way, as well, I could keep contributing to my RRSP. And, of course, I already owned everything outright that I needed to enjoy my present lifestyle. So retirement at 35 was not only possible but also reasonably secure. I already had close to $20,000 in my RRSP. The only thing I really needed to do was build up my nonregistered portfolio.

During 1993, I began investing in bank funds. I was looking for a better return than the cash instruments were paying. Although I still kept half my money in GICs and government bonds, I ventured into a combination of total equity, balanced, and bond mutual funds. In my first foray into equity-type investments, I felt safer buying bank funds because to me banks were part of a solid, conservative institution, and I thought that would be reflected in the makeup of their fund families. I believed better diversification for a relatively small investment was also a good idea.

But I got caught on a bond fund. The stated rates on all the separate bonds within the fund were higher than what I could have received buying bonds on my own. I thought that, since the fund invested in interest-bearing instruments, I could count on a return generally based on the average of these rates. I asked the bank representative if my thinking was logical, and she agreed, but she added there was another dimension to the fund. If interest rates went down, the unit value of the fund would increase, and if interest rates went up, the unit value would decrease. I told her I thought rates were increasing, so didn't that mean I shouldn't be buying that bond fund? She looked down at all the paperwork we had just gone through and didn't answer. Then I said, "But I should be able to count on the higher rates of return within the fund to keep the value up, right?" She nodded her head in agreement and said, "But the funds will fluctuate." I should have done more research until I really understood bond funds. Instead, I purchased the fund and watched the value go down. I was right that interest rates were going up, but that was no consolation. I cut my losses and got out of the fund.

This loss reminded me of a time in the early 1980s when I read some doomsday money books warning of impending world financial chaos. Those "experts" advised buying gold to survive the coming triple-digit inflation and monetary collapse. I thought owning a few gold coins and bars, just in case, couldn't hurt. I was wrong. Although I purchased the gold well after its 1979 high of over $950 an ounce, I still paid about $400 per ounce and held on to that security blanket far too long, earning no return whatsoever. When I finally smartened up and sold it all, I suffered a loss of $1,800. The fact that 75% of the loss could be used to offset a capital gain was no consolation either.

I was investing $1,000 a month in 1994 just before leaving my job with the realtor. Real estate was still in a slump, and that office was a stressful place to be, so I left the job as summer approached.

My next job was in the accounts department of a local hospital. Although I found the working conditions intolerable, I stayed there to build up my freedom fund. My coworkers said that, whenever there was a vacancy posted for their department, it was always filled by someone from outside the hospital. I wasn't surprised. I left after nine months, graciously creating an opening for some other poor fool.

Although the goal of financial freedom was uppermost in my mind, I fell into the trap of rewarding myself while I stayed in that horrible job. But it wasn't in the form of easily identified consumer luxury goods such as jewellery, clothes, vacations, or entertainment. For me, it was in the form of spending money on home improvements.

There was a massive old tree, much too close to the house, that I paid about $1,000 to have cut down and removed. Then I had three dozen new trees and a handful of bushes brought in to give my backyard some creative form and privacy. I hired students to help me tear out the grass, dig up new beds, and plant the various flowering bushes, cedars, and willows. I bought a new stove and a new dishwasher. Then I had a central vacuum and a burglar alarm installed.

So I kept working. I loved the house and the upgrades, and it was the first time I decorated for my pleasure, not for resale. I had one bedroom turned into a library for my extensive collection of old books, which continued to grow. Beautifully bound volumes lined the wall-to-wall shelving, but I'd bought most of the books for a dollar each from garage sales, library book sales, or flea markets. I had a completely new kitchen, a new bathroom, and new broadloom throughout — everything looked new. Work might have been hellish, but my home was heavenly.

It wasn't only the compensation or "I deserve it" trap that kept me from earlier financial freedom. I think that, as I got closer to my early retirement deadline, I became apprehensive about taking that big step. I truly wanted to be free, but I'd never done it before. Or maybe I was just on a final spending spree trying to buy everything I thought I wouldn't be able to purchase after I left regular employment. I also think that cultural conditioning made it difficult to plunge into an alternative lifestyle. I didn't know any 35-year-old retirees to call on to calm my anxieties.

As I reached my 35th birthday, I was still on the fence. After a bad winter, my driveway and front porch needed major repairs, so I hired a contractor to fix both and decided to work a little longer. I also rented out one room in my home to another student for the 1995–96 term to supplement my savings.

After my job at the hospital, I found work with an insurance broker. This turned out to be a good education in the area of consumer insurance products. I also gained an inside perspective on the claims process when my house was robbed and my car stolen. Those experiences along with on-the-job knowledge led me to confidently bypass the insurance broker and choose future policies with a discount insurer instead.

By 1996, my financial picture was looking good. I added a canvas awning to the front of the house but couldn't think of any other improvements to make. There would be more yard and gardening work to do, but landscaping was a hobby of mine and something to look forward to when I was retired. The housing market was recovering, and I watched the value of my home gradually increase. My net worth was $225,000, but I continued to work. Finally, a very sad event nudged me into retirement.

For most of my life, I've lived near my family. Part of the reason I made an offer on my first house was that it sat across the street from my aunt's home. It was comforting to know that if anything went wrong I could just run across the road. In fact, when I initially couldn't sleep in my spooky house, I spent the nights on her sofa bed. Even though my aunt was self-supporting all her life, there were problems with her various jobs, and in later years she was miserable at work. When she turned 65 and retired, the change in her personality was remarkable. She was cheerful all the time. She happily went on outings with friends, participated in many volunteer activities, was quick to help our family, and enjoyed new hobbies. She loved being retired! Sadly, her health failed, and, after only a few years of joyful freedom, she died.

Her death made me realize that life really is too short. I felt so sad that she spent most of her life working long and hard for the reward of a happy retirement, which in the end was simply too little, too late.

After 15 years of working, I quit and retired at 36.

FREEDOM FACTORS

- Eliminate the mortgage and don't take on any new debt.
- Determine cash flow and income needs for both phases of retirement: before and after age 65.
- Contribute to an RRSP in January for that calendar year.
- Build a substantial and diversified net worth.
- Look for income from all sources.
- Research alternatives in all areas: investment

products, regular expenditures, assets for net worth, major purchases.

- Gather as many "expert" opinions as possible for any financial plan or transaction, then do your own research and make your own decisions.
- Don't use fleeting rewards or fear of freedom to keep you in the rat race.
- Spend less time making a living and more time making a life.

CHAPTER SIX

PLUNGE INTO FREEDOM

After I made the decision, it was the most wonderful feeling to finally retire. When I was finishing up the last few weeks at the insurance company, a coworker congenially said, "You don't have to look so happy. You're positively glowing." I couldn't wait for the two weeks to end, and I felt no remorse over leaving my employer. I never have.

My first day of freedom began slowly. I slept late into the chilly morning. After I finally got up, I leisurely prepared a breakfast of broiled grapefruit sprinkled with brown sugar and blueberry pancakes made from scratch. Earl Grey tea in a Chintzware teapot completed the tray laid with Irish linen, sterling silver, and antique Blue Willow china. After breakfast, I took a stroll through the quiet neighbourhood, surprised at all I'd missed while trudging off to work during the months before. At noon, I met a friend at a trendy local café, both of us feeling like "ladies who lunch." In the afternoon, I went with a friend to a book sale. We arrived just as it started, well before any working people could get there, and eyed every title, scooping up some real treasures. Later we had an impromptu dinner back at my house, happily discussing our finds from the sale. After supper, we moved into the living room to enjoy a roaring fire. We had another glass of wine while the embers in the fireplace glowed gold, then red. Simple abundance. Simply perfect.

Later I reviewed the events of my pleasurable day. But it wasn't just one day. Or a week. Or a month. It was my new lifestyle. I was retired. I was free. I was a woman of independent means. Well, maybe not means, but independent certainly.

My net worth was about $225,000 at retirement. Of that amount, the house was $150,000, based on recent comparable sales in the area. If I kept the formulated $20,000 in my RRSP, then I had only $55,000 to finance the early retirement period, not the advised $80,000. I could have gone back to work for a couple of years to cover the shortfall, but that wasn't a palatable idea. I liked the retirement experience too much.

I began wondering just how correct those required amounts were, so I tried another "expert" formula I'd come across. It showed that I'd need $160,000 to finance the next 30 years! That figure was based on the assumptions that an inflation rate of three percent would apply to my yearly cost of living and that a rate of return of six percent could be expected before taxes. It wasn't clear if the formula factored in different income tax brackets in its calculations or not. I've found that many of these formulas assume a tax bracket of 40%, but my taxes would be close to zero. So the wide disparity in the nest egg needed between the first formula and this one resulted from guessing all the variables in each. I couldn't see how recommendations that produced a difference of $80,000 could be construed as guidelines. According to some financial wizards, I needed $80,000, but then again I might need $160,000. Guidelines like that weren't very helpful. How could I know that I wouldn't need $260,000? I couldn't know, and neither could anyone else, no matter how much of an "expert." No one can know future financial numbers for the economy or for an individual. I decided that the best way to determine my needs in retirement would simply be to live it or try it out. Only by doing it would I really know.

If it turned out that my savings were deficient, I could simply get a job. Even so, I'd have enjoyed many years of blissful freedom. Then after working for a short period, I'd have many more years of freedom ahead.

But I still had other options. If the future did confirm the three percent inflation rate, the six percent return rate, and the $160,000 savings requirement, I could live well from the $55,000 capital and future gains for about 10 years and then work for the remaining 20 years. Not an attractive idea. Or I could remain retired for the full 30 years if I sold my house and lived in a $45,000 co-op apartment or rural cottage. On the other hand, if the $80,000 guideline turned out to be more accurate, I could either move to a $125,000 house, providing the $25,000 shortfall, or keep my home and earn some income from work I enjoyed, or I could even work full time for a couple of years.

However, if neither formula accurately predicted my financial future, under the most catastrophic financial conditions (runaway inflation, deflation, market collapse, or personal disability) I'd still be in a sound position because of my economical cost of living (no debts, low taxes, liquid and major assets, and self-sufficient lifestyle). I knew that in retirement I'd spend a lot of time following the economy and structuring my investments conservatively in relation to the changing financial environment. And I could always work, sell assets, or, in the worst case, apply for government assistance. I considered every disastrous scenario I could think of, but there was always an acceptable solution. The most important aspect of financial devastation, though, was its likelihood. Actuarial science was the discipline I'd so carefully avoided, but it had a useful application now. Insurance companies rely on actuaries to provide statistics to help determine the level of insurer risk and probable claims settlements or annuity payment amounts. Considering my standard of living, net worth, and personal resourcefulness, I was well prepared for a potential monetary setback. In facing a major financial problem, I'd still be better off than most, all circumstances considered, but the chance of that happening was slim. I had conservative investments. I had liability and property insurance. I didn't have disability insurance, which covers the loss of income from the inability to work, since I wasn't working and therefore didn't have employment income that needed to be insured. However, I researched the need for extra health insurance, weighing the statistical probabilities and my personal level of health in assessing the risk.

Much more likely, though, was the other extreme, where I wouldn't have to make any grave changes throughout my early retirement period and would probably increase my net worth. Since I'd spend more time on my hobby of investing, I expected better returns, if only from monitoring my portfolios on a more regular basis. And I knew I wouldn't be spending all my time at pursuits that didn't generate income. I still wanted the social aspect of employment, but only for a few hours a week, and I wanted to be involved in an endeavour I enjoyed. I'd been a volunteer for a few years but had become disappointed with the low level of satisfaction I felt compared with the time and effort I'd spent. Surely I could find a way of helping others and receive some small remuneration at the same time. I completely expected my financial position not only to endure but also to improve. In fact, over the first four years of my early retirement, it did just that.

I went from a net worth of $225,000 in 1996 to total assets of about $300,000 by the summer of 2000. Of that amount, my house had increased in value by only $20,000. The majority of the growth came from investment returns, other asset appreciation, and additional savings.

In retirement, I've spent more time researching different types of investments and analysing statement data on individual companies and the contents of mutual funds. I've read far more personal finance books, magazines, and newspapers than before, and I've tuned in to radio and television money programs more often. It's been rewarding simply because I've had the extra time. I've also had some uplifting jobs that generated a little employment income. For the first two years, I worked only as a favour for friends, covering their absences when needed. I also worked during a municipal election for a new fun experience. Then, at the end of 1998, I landed a dream job. Being an avid reader, I couldn't have been offered a more ideal job than at my neighbourhood library. The part-time hours were somewhat more than I wanted, but it was such a great environment to be in that I quickly accepted the job. My retirement employment earnings to that point were about $4,400. The library income to the end of 1999 totalled $9,900 since I'd helped during a staff shortage by adding extra hours. In 2000, however, I was able to reduce the time substantially. For the year, my employment earnings were $5,600, and now I continue to work only three hours a week. I didn't want to leave such a perfect workplace entirely, but there were new things I wanted to do. It was the kind of dilemma I'd always hoped for in retirement — a fulfilling fun job that I never wanted to quit versus so many other enjoyable ways to spend my time.

With employment income, though, I've been able to keep contributing to my RRSP and carry forward the deduction to use against future income. That way, if I ever earn more than the tax-free threshold, I can reduce my earnings with any available tax credits first and then use as little of the amount carried forward as needed to bring my income below the nontaxable limit. Given the choice, I'd rather not pay tax.

In addition, when my expenses were lower than I'd planned, I added the savings to my nonregistered portfolio. I've also been able to reinvest capital returns because I've been living within my part-time income means for over a year now. Even though the library paycheque is diminished, I expect my next fun endeavour to generate some cash flow as well. The important point, though, isn't that I'm still working in retirement. I believe I'll be working for the rest of my life, whether it's in the garden, on the ballet barre, at the piano, in an art studio, or on the computer. The freedom is in working whenever, wherever, and at whatever I choose — the income is a bonus.

I recognize that how I decide to spend my time could be quite different from someone else's choice. But having the freedom to make that enjoyable decision is the most worthwhile part of retirement.

Being retired at such an early age has provided a great amount of personal satisfaction. I think it's the best lifestyle in the world. And, as long as other people share my viewpoint, it would be a mistake to keep my method of finding freedom to myself. I admit that I would feel pleased and gratified (okay, smug) if I could steer others out of the rat-race ruts they've fallen into. But reading about how I did it is one thing. Applying the techniques to your own set of circumstances is quite another. That's what the second part of this book is about.

Some of my ideas are new, but many of the rules I used can be found in similar forms in other books. Regardless, I've presented the methods outlined in this book because they work. But no one can make them work for you. To be of any benefit to you, the knowledge must be used. For example, in the area of moral values, most people know what's right and what's wrong. The proof, however, is in actually doing the right thing. Likewise, most people know what they need to do financially. But the results can only come from doing it. It's not simple, but, like any new task, with practice it becomes easier and faster.

When I was first asked for my advice on achieving financial freedom, I was deluged with reasons (excuses, really) why people can't do it. I know the trials people face in various circumstances. I also know my basic financial plan is universal in getting results. The difficulty stems from applying it. Reading about it is entirely different from putting it into practice.

So the rest of the book provides techniques for you to stop being a spectator and start being a player. The money concepts described in the first part flow through the next chapters as gentle reminders, helping to fix the knowledge in your subconscious. The new information shows you how to apply that knowledge to everyday life.

Faced with imposing obstacles, I tend to confront them directly. My natural or inherited response is to overcome any deterrents to my dreams. I believe this can be a learned behaviour. When I was being interviewed for a national newspaper, the journalist asked me if I thought others can achieve such an early retirement. My response was an emphatic "Definitely." A month later, when I was being filmed for a financial television program, the producer asked me the same question. I told her, "I think almost anyone can do what I've done. It's not how much you earn, it's what you do with what you have. It's a skill, an attitude, and a commitment. Combined with action and perseverance, it can produce astounding results."

Everybody has problems. How you deal with your own problems will determine your ultimate success. Get a better attitude and find better answers. I achieved financial freedom by challenging deterrents with "But I want it. Other people have it. Why *not* me?"

Why not you?

CHAPTER SEVEN

A NEW ATTITUDE

By yourself, as a couple, or as a family, you must look after your own interests and desires from this day forward. You have to stop supporting all the individuals and groups in society that keep you from being financially free. You and the people you love must come first. Before you even think of giving to other important causes, address your own priorities. One time, when I felt sorry that I couldn't give more to a certain charity, a wise relative said, "You can't look after all the dogs and cats of the world," and figuratively speaking she was right. So, instead of cash, I gave my time and donated clothing and household goods. You must keep in mind that as far as money is concerned charity begins at home.

If you add it all up, you'd be amazed at the amount of cash you've spent automatically over the years, unconsciously increasing someone else's profits. All the products and services that didn't give you value for your money paid for someone else's lifestyle and added to government coffers. Exorbitant income taxes for the privilege of working pay for government programs, salaries, and debt. And by accepting government statistical biases, media-influenced culture, and "expert" advice, you are swayed into exchanging your money for a false sense of security or public standing. You become a follower and purchaser of others' lifestyle choices, which aren't necessarily your own. Statistics Canada supplies data on low income and average wage rates, enabling you to measure yourself in the income-level competition. I was told by a StatsCan clerk that they don't gather information on levels of happiness.

In fact, Jonathan Chevreau of the *Financial Post* reviewed Michael Adams's book *Better Happy than Rich?* and noted that the book shows the difference in levels of happiness between Canadians earning $20,000 to $30,000 and those earning $70,000 to $80,000 is negligible. Only when earnings exceed $80,000 a year do feelings of happiness change, because people have more freedom of choice. It seems to me, then, that it's not just having money but also having the opportunity to choose a desired lifestyle that gives true happiness. Hedonism. Does big money buy it? Not necessarily. But governments and commercial enterprises would have you believe that it does. A higher income means higher taxes as well as a greater potential to buy more and expensive products.

Both governments and corporations stand to gain more revenue through advertising and entertainment. The media create cultural ideals for mesmerized individuals to dream of and supposedly attain through purchase. It is in these outside groups' best financial interests to encourage your desire for higher income since it results not only in higher taxes and increased spending for consumer goods but also in a greater need for "expert" services. All levels of government; large corporations and small businesses; financial products, insurance, and real estate salespeople; lawyers and accountants — they all take a bigger chunk of your hard-earned income as a result of the "more is better" culture. They reap the rewards, but are you getting your money's worth?

The good news is that you now have the tools to craft your own financial security and a much quicker retirement. The bad news is that, while it's easy to read the rules, it's much harder to follow them. But if you learn to recognize the deterrents to wealth, challenge them, and take action, you will be on a faster track toward early retirement. And there's more good news: in everyday financial matters, most people are already doing some things right, or at least they know what they're doing wrong. If you're in the Boomer generation, you likely won't be starting with nothing. You probably already have a home, a car, furnishings, appliances, some luxury goods, and possibly some savings and investments. You may be in your peak earning years. Regardless, you'll have some experience handling money, and, if an existing financial skill is working well, continue to use it.

This book will help you to correct problems and add techniques to accelerate your retirement, and it offers solutions and options along with their documented results. Building a good financial foundation starts with research, analysis, and understanding, which will allow you to formulate your own expert opinion. You will discover a lot of conflicting advice from various financial sources, but in the end only you can decide what will serve your needs best.

The average person probably won't want to spend as much time as I do on finances and investing, but efficient home economics is still your first priority, which this book covers in detail. Then, once you've maximized your cash position, you'll have money to invest. I'll discuss investing in a later chapter, but there are many other books that focus solely on this huge financial area. If you have the interest, read some of these investment tomes to further your financial education. My main concern is to ensure that you reach the enviable position of having money to invest. To accomplish this feat, you will need the skills to accelerate cash flow as well as the techniques to detour around financial roadblocks.

Major obstacles to building wealth include taxation, debt, socialized spending, cultural statistics, learned behaviours, and personal attitudes. Contrary to popular belief, it's not the amount of money you earn that determines wealth accumulation — it's how you manage the money you have. And wealth isn't dependent on receiving a windfall. It's how you handle all the money you do acquire that matters most.

As mentioned in *The Millionaire Next Door*, by Thomas Stanley and William Danko, most millionaires did not inherit their wealth. Their fortunes came from budgeting: keeping expenses far lower than income and investing the savings. Most of them were self-employed and took advantage of the favourable tax treatment. Almost every millionaire was a mortgage-free homeowner and had lived in the same house for over 20 years. Most were married with children. On average, they spent about eight hours a month making their own investment decisions, budgeted carefully (saving at least 15%–20% of net income), bought assets that appreciated, admitted to being frugal, and resisted hiring others when they could do the work themselves, and over half of them never paid more than $30,000 for a car. These facts show how the self-made millionaires really became rich.

To manage money more effectively for yourself, then, you need to follow the millionaires' financial habits. Behaviour is shaped by attitude, which in turn is reflected by an individual's reactions to the outside world. Therefore, your attitude, or how you choose to react to events, is the most important aspect in creating beneficial habits and hurdling money obstacles. Your level of wealth partially depends on how well you handle the deterrents to accumulating money. Likewise, how well you handle these impediments depends entirely on your attitude.

Psychological barriers to financial freedom take many forms and are usually harder to identify than obvious hindrances such as taxes and debt. On an emotional level, your family may be against your goal of early retirement simply because they have no experience in achieving it themselves and fear anything new and untried. They may reason that, since they haven't done it, you can't do it either. Or your immediate family may be afraid of living in deprivation. Give them a copy of my book. Even after you're retired, you may continue to face adverse family reactions, as I did. I'd enjoyed my freedom for more than a year, but one relative still shook her head in wonder and concluded that I was "just plain lazy," while another still told others that I couldn't *get* a job. They didn't understand what I was doing or why, and from their frames of reference they had to create reasons for my lifestyle they could comprehend. My parents were the first to accept my retirement when they saw I was leading an independent, blissful existence, urban middle-class style. Others applauded my success only after my early retirement attracted media attention. So realize that you are working toward a financial goal for yourself and your closest loved ones. When you are retired and have a lot more time to help or visit with other family and friends, they will be happy for you then.

More importantly, be aware of your own sabotaging responses, such as "I can't," "I can't be bothered," "What will others think?" and "What if . . . ?" These are learned attitudes that will keep you from reaching any goal. Challenge counterproductive thoughts with contrary answers. Naturally, "I can't" becomes "Sure! Why not?" If people spent the same time creating ways to accomplish a goal as they did thinking of reasons why they can't, they'd achieve a lot more. Combat negativity by going ahead and doing it anyway.

The "I can't be bothered" attitude is a huge barrier to early retirement. To all the people who can't be bothered to pursue their financial dreams, I say, "I can't be bothered to schlep off to work every day." I think it takes much more time and effort to be a taxed-to-death, money-grubbing, trend-following, meaningless-possession-hoarding, overly encumbered work slave, heeling to the commands of your masters, than it does to choose and follow your goal of freedom. Harsh? No. If you really want to be free, then you have to recognize the causes of your enslavement and make the effort to break the chains.

I've already discussed the "What will others think?" deterrent. They will always think what they like whether you know it or not. Know what counts for you. Everybody has an opinion, but everybody shouldn't matter. Remember, when you succeed, those who said you couldn't will be the first ones to say they knew you could. People like to be right and will develop a "selective memory" if needed. To deal with what people think, develop a couple of beneficial variations of that trait: "selective sight" and "selective hearing." Don't waste your breath when faced with naysayers shaking their heads or furrowing their brows. When you're in selective mode, though, don't forget to nod and smile.

I believed at a young age that I'd be free to do whatever I wanted in life. Then later, as a teenager, I was sheltered from the negative adult experiences that seem to squelch childhood dreams and desires. Because of my limited worldly experience, I didn't believe in failure, so my goals endured. Still, it's much more likely that you as an adult reader will be successful because you'll have the benefit of my experience, the techniques that work, and the proof that if you believe you can, and if you make a commitment to persevere, you'll achieve financial freedom, as I have.

The difficulty with the psychological barrier of "What if . . . ?" is that you can never win. If the feared circumstance happens, then it's a problem. But while experience can be the toughest teacher, it is possibly the best. It's hard to imagine progress ever taking place if people are immobilized by "What if . . . ?" There is risk in everyday life. There is risk in taking early retirement. You minimize it by having both money and insurance. How much of each you'll need leads us to the next roadblock.

Experts can help you to reach your financial goals, but they can also impede your progress. They are not infallible. They do not have all the answers. And they will never be as concerned about your wealth as you are. Yet they have their place in the wealth-building process. Financial services professionals are privy to financial data and provide access to a vast array of products. Many are knowledgeable in their fields as well. But you must differentiate between fact and opinion. This is where your own research, analysis, and understanding come in. Professional advisors know the terms that identify economic events and relationships as well as the industry jargon for financial services and products. Some have accreditation in personal finance. However, they cannot forecast future economic conditions with accuracy; they can only make "educated guesses" using certain variables and historical data. In my experience, these "guestimates" are of questionable benefit. When economic conditions change, I've seen their past incorrect assumptions simply referred to as "outdated." Don't put your faith in financial fortune tellers.

We've already looked at the limitations of a few "expert" retirement equations. Tracy LeMay of the *Financial Post* investigated on-line retirement formulas and, using a sample personal profile, discovered that results varied widely. While a major bank's calculator determined that the existing yearly contribution of $10,000 could be reduced to about $6,660 a year, a financial services company recommended that savings be increased by more than $26,000 every year in order to reach the same retirement goal. Similarly, an article published in *Worth Magazine* discussed conventional retirement calculators "like those found on many investment Web sites" and stated that ". . . most of the planning tools we use are virtually useless." I chose to retire even though I didn't have the sum recommended by either of the differing professional formulas I found. As it turned out, though, I enjoyed a much wider spread between earnings and expenses than the experts assumed. It wasn't luck. Anyone who had followed my methods of cash flow control and put savings in conservatively balanced investments would have received a real rate of return far surpassing the experts' educated guess of three percent a year.

Using incorrect assumptions to calculate the percentage of current income required after retirement can result in a much greater amount amassed at retirement than will be needed for a yearly income. As well, most money formulas calculate a lump sum of capital that will still be intact at the person's time of death as part of the estate and will be taxed as income and then forwarded to any heirs, whether they need it or not. One of my friends said that it was as if her heirs would profit from her death. And look at what's happening to retired people today: according to one insurance company providing RRIFs, 60% of people taking the regulated minimum withdrawals from their plans wished they had the option of taking out less. The amounts simply weren't needed or wanted and resulted in "clawbacks." The people ended up paying much higher taxes on portions of the withdrawals they didn't even want.

The percentage of income needed in retirement that some experts are advising ranges from 60% to 80% of current gross income. Apparently, this formula factors in decreased costs as a result of eliminating work-related expenses, children leaving home, and the mortgage being paid off. It's not clear if the effects of taxation (clawbacks, changed tax brackets) have been factored in. And what about the effects of widespread seniors' discounts — from travel costs to banking services? Does that range assume all retired people will live the same currently full-priced lifestyle (new vehicles financed or leased every few years, record consumer debt levels, aggressive savings, a family-sized home, cottage, or boat)? Does the formula allow for the vitality of Boomer retirees who will likely be involved in income-producing consulting, hobbies, or other activities?

In a recent magazine article, one financial professional advised that a $750,000 interest-bearing investment (in current dollars) would equal a $45,000 yearly income, allowing a lifestyle of dinner out a few times a week, a golf or tennis membership, and some adult education courses. The planner assumed annual interest of six percent on the savings. There was no mention of the effects of inflation, pensions, or taxes. The planner also assumed that the retiree would want to leave the entire $750,000 along with the rest of the estate intact after death for the heirs and the tax man. If a 45 year old were to follow that advice today, scrambling and scrimping, striving for a retirement stash of $750,000, what kind of lifestyle would that allow over the next 20 years? To accumulate a present value of $750,000, using the experts' real rate of return of three percent (six percent return minus three percent inflation), a person would have to save more than $3,000 every month for the next 20 years.

"Experts" and their crystal ball calculations are doomed to supply flawed information for a number of reasons. Figures based on assumptions about future values for the variables in a formula can only be approximate at best. Using gross income as the main part of the equation results only in gross miscalculations. A general formula with arbitrary values is irrelevant in predicting a specific individual's or couple's future needs. For this purpose, expressing future values in present dollars adds to the complexity, confusion, and degree of error. However, the retirement numbers do create demand for financial products and services. If the expert's figures show you'll need $750,000, as opposed to $250,000, then there will be more profits in sales and commissions for those in the financial industry. Could there be an unconscious bias for experts to motivate consumers to buy as many mutual funds, stocks, bonds, and term deposits as they can sell?

Having a huge retirement fund also parallels the "more is better" culture, but is it better when it comes at the expense of present living conditions? Will the financial hardship, long working hours, frustration, struggle, and exhaustion be worth the debatable peace of mind? This is an example of the experts profiting from the "What if . . . ?" thinking. "What if you won't have enough to live in retirement? What if you won't have enough to live *well* in retirement?" The insurance industry has been profiting a long time from the "What if . . . ?" obstacle to building wealth. "What if you contract an illness or develop a disability, have property damage or loss, or are sued? What if you die prematurely?" But think about this: what if the financial products you buy are a waste of money?

What if you don't need expensive insurance policies or any-where near the fortune the experts advise? What if you're forced to take out more money than you want or need from your RRIF and squander so much in tax? What if you can provide for your family and save for the future better than the financial services industry can, keeping its high fees and commissions for yourself instead of lining its pockets? All of these possibilities should be considered alongside any outcome that an insurance agent or financial planner suggests to you. The solution? Deal with the present first. Insure yourself against the hardship of possible losses in the present, not against every kind of potential loss in the future. Don't suffer need-lessly now based on an expert's guess; instead, make a better prediction of your future by tackling your here and now.

Your cost of living in retirement will depend on how you choose to spend your money at that time. Contrary to common planning formulas, the focus should be on future expenses and should not depend on any gross income figure before retirement. Not only does your income likely change from year to year, but so can the effects of taxation, varying the amount of your net income each year. It's the net or dis-posable income that is actually available for savings, servicing debt, unusual outlays, luxuries, and living expenses. And these cost proportions will vary depending on individual or family circumstances, goals, and desires. Examining your current expenditures as opposed to income, then, provides a far more accurate prediction of your retirement cost of living. My retire-ment lifestyle turned out to be only 40% of my average gross income. As an example of the degree of variance even on my modest salary, costs have turned out to be 25% of my highest gross income and 50% of my lowest. That illustrates a 25% spread depending on when the calculations were made, not to mention a large difference from the experts' recommended 60%–80% of gross earnings required. If I'd followed the experts' suggestions, I'd still be needlessly chained to a job.

An analysis of expenses during my working life provided me with a much more useful prediction of future retirement figures. Once I became mortgage free and chose better-value housing, my total cost of living decreased by 46%. Since I've been retired, my costs have continued to fall four percent a year, which has allowed more luxury purchases and savings. While my own consumer price index has been falling, Statistics Canada's calculated inflation rate has been increasing at an average of 1.5% per year from 1996 to 1999. This is yet another example of how general figures don't accurately reflect individual retiree circumstances.

To understand this difference, I researched exactly how the consumer price index (CPI) reflects inflation levels. The government derives the CPI by measuring the change in price of a "market basket" of goods and services that people buy. Utilities and other costs of living are factored in, along with seasonal adjustments, to provide base costs for the market basket. Note, however, that the same items are included in the same quantities each time prices are recorded. That method doesn't reflect the likelihood that consumers will either buy fewer of the market basket items or buy substitutes when prices rise. It also ignores the segment of the population that never purchases one or more of the market basket products and services. If you're not spending money on all those consumables in the same quantity and at the same regularity, or you're not purchasing them at all, then the inflation rate will vary in its relevance to your personal purchasing power now or in retirement. In *Your Guide to the CPI*, StatsCan acknowledges that the data it supplies isn't a cost-of-living index and doesn't match the experiences of any particular household. So an average government inflation rate used in a financial planning formula won't necessarily reflect your future cost of living.

As well, how much an individual or family is able to spend on a market basket of goods determines whether they are classified as living in poverty or not. When I discovered that StatsCan labelled me as "poor" because of my spending and income levels in retirement, I decided to research the rationale behind such a categorization. Poor? Me? By no stretch of the imagination do I live in a state of poverty. Once again, gross income levels are used to grossly misrepresent standards of living. I also found out that there is much debate over the "poverty line," which is now referred to as the "low income cut-off level." In a 1999 StatsCan report, the poverty line was at an income of $16,000 for a single person living in a large city. My current income is well below that figure, yet, through clever money management, savings and investments, no mortgage or any other debt, tax concessions (thanks to the government's "poor folk" classification), I live a comfortable middle-class lifestyle without having to work. It seems that the government formulates its own assumptions that result in very misleading statistics.

A good example was a discussion paper from the National

Council of Welfare (winter 1998–99) that presented many research groups' differing statistics using the "basket of goods" spending statistics instead of the gross income approach alone. The most interesting finding was the wide range of total expenditure figures that classified the poorest 20% of Canadian families. Depending on the organization, the average family was categorized as poor if it spent anywhere from $19,800 to $30,500 per year. In my case, as a single person, spending less than $11,000 a year put me in the classification of poor. Interesting. With a net worth of around $300,000, I'm labelled poor. Yet another single person who earns $30,000 a year, spends $30,000 a year, and has a negative cash flow and net worth (expenses and debts outweighing income, savings, and assets) would not be considered poor. Who's really poor: a low-income, low-debt, low spender or a high-income, high-debt, high spender?

Furthermore, in determining the poverty level by measuring consumption through spending, the government interprets from its data that I need to buy paper towels, paper napkins, plastic wrap, fabric softener, floor wax, disposable scouring pads, large plastic garbage bags, a daily newspaper, and cable television. As well, it suggests that I should spend at least $500 a year on recreation, $800 for gifts, and over $400 on miscellaneous expenses (including $250 for gambling, debt charges, and bank fees) to have the minimum acceptable standard of living. I don't adhere to those ecologically harmful spending habits or those arbitrary purchase amounts, and I don't buy those products, so by the government's findings I must be destitute!

It seems that it's not what you *have* but what you *earn*,

what you repeatedly *buy*, and how much you *spend* that determines your financial class. According to committees, activists, and the government, wealth doesn't determine it; income level and consumption do. I may have drawers full of towels and fabric napkins, but since I don't buy disposable ones I'm branded as poor. Since I don't rent television service (cable) but own it (TV tower), I'm considered poor. I have an environmentally friendly garbage can but don't buy big black garbage bags, so I'm labelled poor. And because I don't pay bank fees or service any debt, I'm poor? Once again, let's take a look at self-made millionaires. They are rich. How did they achieve their "rich" status? It's not how much they *earn*, and it's not how much they *spend*; in fact, it's the difference between the two and how much they *have*. Government propaganda versus laughing-all-the-way-to-the-bank millionaires' methodology. Which group do you want to emulate: bureaucrats or millionaires?

By now, you're beginning to see how ludicrous general statistics, formulas, and so-called expert opinions can be. The following chapters will show you exactly how you can live a rich lifestyle on less money than you think simply by evaluating your expenditures. That focus will lead you to establish genuine priorities, live within your means, forecast future needs, build wealth, and retire early. For now, be aware of the psychological and authoritative barriers that can hinder your progress toward financial freedom.

The daily bombardment of advertising is another obstacle to overcome. Marketers are masters at influencing your psyche and shaping your money-handling behaviour. They play on your emotions, inducing you to make their desired buyer response. While people are aware of being swayed into media-prompted purchases on occasion, the most financially detrimental selling ploys are those that result in automatic or repeat buying and those that satisfy the "have it now," "you deserve it," and "more is better" subliminal messages. We are living in an era when mass marketing, media, and entertainment have superimposed a culture of consumerism as the societal norm. If you don't wish for certain items, you don't fit in. If you don't buy a certain number of products, you are lacking. If you don't have some kind of debt, you are a minority. Yet millionaires are not status seekers and don't waste money on assets that don't appreciate. They abhor debt. Ironically, they are also a minority — one that most aspire to.

Have it now? Choose financial freedom now. As for early retirement — you deserve it. More is better? More time, more choice, more joy. They're better than anything.

Have you noticed the recent change in advertising to reflect this trend? Campaigns for lotteries, credit cards, and financial planning are shifting their focus from the wealth of things to the wealth of time. Unfortunately, though, over the past 50 years, consumers have been influenced to adopt such poor money-handling habits that they'll achieve the financial freedom they want only by changing their attitudes toward spending.

Overconsumption and relaxed attitudes toward debt accumulation have contributed to massive consumer debt problems in Canada. Personal bankruptcies have soared; debt levels have become higher than income levels. This is a serious problem for all Canadians who want financial freedom. You won't be free while you have debt. If you make credit payments, you need income to cover them over and above your daily costs of living. If you are encumbered with lease payments, mortgage payments, loan payments, and credit card payments, and you continue to live beyond your means, you'll be tied to a job. At one time, a debtor's prison really did exist. If you couldn't pay your debts, you were put in jail. Times have changed, and so has the stigma attached to debt and bankruptcy. Although piling up credit and declaring bankruptcy are so much easier today, neither one is the way to financial freedom.

If you want to be free, you must become financially secure. To become financially secure, you must cultivate wealth-building habits. Confronting obstacles is your first line of defence. Then knowing the basic rules becomes your strategy. You know how I did it. You know how the millionaires did it. Now you need to know how you can do it.

MILLIONAIRE MIND-SET
- Be aware of psychological barriers to freedom.
- Don't follow externally conditioned consumer behaviours.
- Question "expert" advice.
- Research, think, and become your own expert.
- Judge statistics as relevant or irrelevant to *your* life.
- Recognize the roadblocks to building wealth and overcome them.

CHAPTER EIGHT

FINDING YOURSELF

Building wealth follows some simple principles. The two most basic are live well below your means and invest the surplus. But you can't know what your "means" are unless you have a good grasp of the total net funds you have coming in. Similarly, you can't discern what "well below" is unless you determine your total cash outlay. And you can only invest a surplus when there is more money coming in than going out.

A personal *Income and Expense Statement* shows cash flow over a set period of time. It can reflect all transactions during a year, but starting with a monthly record is easier. Net income is money received from all sources less corresponding deductions. This figure equals your means. Expenses indicate the outflows of cash. When total expenditures are subtracted from net income, the result shows the degree to which you're living below your means (*if* you are). A surplus results from the proper handling of your home finances. This "profit" is reflected on your personal *Balance Sheet*, which includes assets and liabilities (debts). You need to do both statements initially to determine where you stand, and you should update them yearly to monitor your progress.

> **Simplified Income and Expense Statement**
> **Incoming money - Outgoing money = Wealth(+) or Poverty(-)**
> **Net income - Expenses = Surplus/Profit(+) or Loss(-)**

INCOME AND EXPENSE STATEMENT

Income

To keep it simple, income refers here to all *net* incoming funds. It is your actual paycheque amount plus any other money received from investments, rentals, self-employment, pensions, etc., after deductions. As your means, this figure represents the total amount of money you have available for expenses and building wealth.

Expenses

Basically, these are all the ways you spend your money. Get out your chequebook, credit card and bill statements, tax notices, and any other records that show cash outlays over a typical month. Don't forget to include interest payments on debts and irregular expenditures — divide annual payments by 12, bimonthly ones by six, quarterly ones by four, etc. to calculate the average monthly amount. "Miscellaneous" is the amount of cash not accounted for in the above costs, probably pocket money spent on small items. Track this amount by analysing cash receipts and withdrawals or by taking the difference between cash at the start of the month, less cash at the end, less documented spending (from bill statements and receipts). If miscellaneous spending is a large amount, you need to improve your method of record keeping. The next chapter covers simple techniques for keeping track of cash flow. By focusing your attention on expenses, you become efficient at handling your costs of living, providing for luxuries, and allowing savings to accumulate. I don't suggest including savings as an expense, since the procedure in this book is to categorize expenses based on costs of living, keeping savings separate for building wealth. Savings, or the surplus of income over expenses, are carried over to your Balance Sheet.

A *Balance Sheet* is a statement of your assets and debts at a specific point in time, and the difference between the two is your net worth. (It can also be called a *Statement of Net Worth.*) The surplus from cash flow appears as an increase in assets or a decrease in liabilities. While a surplus always enhances net worth, I believe that net worth can only occur when you own more than you owe. If liabilities (debts) outweigh assets in a business venture, then it's considered a "bad risk." Yet the same situation in personal finance is gently referred to as "having a negative net worth." Since increasing personal net worth is essential to building wealth, a Balance Sheet in home finance should be taken just as seriously as one in business finance.

Simplified Balance Sheet
Owned property - Owed amounts = Wealth(+) or Poverty(-)
Assets - Liabilities = Net worth(+) or No net worth(-)

BALANCE SHEET

Assets

Everything you own is recorded here. It's important to list all assets because you may be richer than you think. However, if the thought of this task keeps you from doing it, at least list all major assets of value and assign a low arbitrary amount for the remaining personal effects. Minor assets have low monetary values and will be of little consequence in determining your current money-handling abilities. I record my major assets in two categories: money and valuable property.

Money

Start by writing down all cash and nonregistered investment amounts. Include bank account balances, money market funds, term deposits, GICs, T-bills, mutual funds, stocks, gold bullion, and any other type of cash instruments or investments. Then list amounts held in RRSPs, pension plans, and any other registered investments.

Property

Record net asset values for any business or rental property you own. Finally, determine a cash value for all personal property, including house, vehicle(s), art, antiques, jewellery, furnishings, and equipment. Market value, not replacement cost, must be used to assign a likely sale price to each item. Check your local newspaper, resale shop, garage sales, or Internet auction sites for the asking prices of similar items to conservatively evaluate your own. Remember, assets are only worth what someone else will pay for them. If you list all your personal belongings, it will take some time, but it will provide a complete inventory suitable for insurance purposes as well as a list of all property that could be converted into cash.

Add everything (the money total and the property total) together for a total asset figure.

Liabilities

Everything you owe is recorded here. Total all credit card balances, loans, and other debt instalment payments, property and income taxes due (up to the Balance Sheet date), alimony, mortgages (home, investment, or recreational), and any other payments owing.

Net Worth

This figure will give you a clear picture of your wealth or lack of it. Subtract your total liabilities from your total assets. If the amount is a healthy positive, you should feel instantly richer. You are that much closer to freedom. If, however, the total is negative, you must start building wealth now.

There are only two ways to expand net worth: increase assets and decrease liabilities. The best results come from doing both in the extreme — that is, continually adding assets and completely eliminating debt. To do that, you'll need to analyse your Income and Expense Statement and Balance Sheet.

Income and Expense Statement Analysis

If your expenses are less than your income, you are on your way to wealth by living below your means and profiting from it. To accelerate financial freedom, though, you'll have to maximize your profit potential. If expenses equal income, you are no doubt proving Parkinson's Law — "work expands so as to fill the time available for its completion" — but I'm applying it in the financial sense — expenditures expand to the full amount of income received. If income doesn't cover expenses, you are operating your household at a loss and living a poverty lifestyle. One dictionary describes poverty as a "Deficiency in amount" and "The state or condition of being poor." The definition of poor is "Having little or no wealth." Since wealth is net worth, a Balance Sheet that shows a deficiency in that area will similarly define your lifestyle as poor.

Balance Sheet Analysis

If you have abundant assets and scant liabilities, you are on your way to financial freedom. Again, accelerating net worth will hasten your freedom. If, however, your assets equal total debt, you are poor by definition of having little or no wealth, as explained above. If liabilities are larger than total assets, you are living a poverty lifestyle. Overspending and accumulating debt will keep you enslaved to a job to pay for your past and/or present style of living beyond your means. You won't stand a chance of having a future of freedom unless you fix your finances fast.

Barring a windfall of money, your net worth will not improve until your Income and Expense Statement shows a profit or surplus. Liquidating some assets to reduce liabilities on your Balance Sheet will have a positive effect on debt but will not change the level of your net worth right away. Eliminating debt is instrumental in the success of my plan, and in the following chapters there are many methods to erase liabilities and increase net worth. The best solution, though, is to use techniques for lowering expenditures without feeling deprived. Even financial "experts" agree that it is far easier to control outflows than inflows of cash. You don't have nearly as much latitude over your income as you do over your expenses.

Still, you should consider alternative methods of improving your stream of income. Early in life, I tried many different ways to generate income. When I was in grade school, I crafted bookmarks and created surprise gift bags, which I sold to my classmates. Later I sold Avon. Perhaps you can turn a craft, hobby, or other sideline into a small business: take your products to work, donate one as a prize for a charity (business name and phone number attached), have a home party, share a booth at a craft show, or sell your items on the Internet. A doctor I knew carved beautiful carousel animals and other folk sculptures as a hobby, which became lucrative when he showed a few of his pieces at a local art gallery. A friend of mine has a second "summer" kitchen in her basement and uses it to teach cake decorating and canning and preserving food. In university, I gave singing lessons. If you have a special interest or skill, consider teaching a class (check local community centres and colleges). And there are many books offering spare-time business ideas. To save time and money, call your nearby library and have the staff set aside a few books for you to pick up.

Take a part-time job to do something fun or to learn something practical. I "worked" at a live theatre hall and convention centre, being paid to see the shows and take food home. I also worked in the kitchen for an organization's monthly lodge meetings, getting paid to eat brunch and have fun (I was the only woman!). I worked for a small corporation for both the money and to learn how to run a business. I took jobs in the real estate and insurance industries for income and to gain insider knowledge. If you want to learn something, find a suitable workplace, take a part-time job there, ask lots of questions, and learn while you earn. If you're only paid minimum wage, that's still better than learning on your own or paying for classes. Even if your only option is to volunteer, the fun, satisfaction, and free learning are better than spending money on social entertainment. Knowledge *is* power. It can provide an income when you "sell" your new skills, and it can increase savings when you do something yourself instead of paying someone else to do it.

You can also rent out space to increase your income. While technically you're offering a service, I've found that this option takes less time and effort. I've rented out a parking spot as well as a room in my home for extra money. You can rent out space or any other asset you have — cottage, trailer (utility or recreational), vacation time-share, boat, sports or other hobby equipment, workshop, or garage. If you have a double garage but park one car in the driveway anyway, you could rent out the vacant space. I know someone who rented his garage to a vintage car owner for a few years and then to a man who kept his convertible sports car off the road every winter.

The combination of multiple streams of income can be a major supplement to your existing paycheque, but your success depends on your existing skills, aptitude, energy level, and time available for extra work and learning. As well, it provides a future benefit, whereas cutting expenses gives an immediate boost to spare cash. And you have virtually complete control in deciding how your money is spent but much less control in setting your income amounts. Focus on living within your means to accumulate money faster and easier.

You, however, are the only person who can control your spending, and a personal Cash Flow Statement is the best tool for charting income and expenses over a short period of time. When I handled daily financial operations for a small business, I created statements to show the company's current cash position and forecasted cash flow over the next three months. Then I made Cash Flow Statements for my home finances. If you create your own 90-day statement, you will have a clear picture of your current and forecasted cash flow. Also, you'll only need to control your cash four times a year. The statement may need periodic revision, but its purpose is to provide peace of mind by knowing how much money you'll have and how much you'll need to meet expenses over the next three months.

It's very simple to chart your money if you have a regular income. Still, I was able to make accurate cash flow forecasts for a real estate office that had variable commissions coming in at irregular times. Fortunately, expenses followed a monthly pattern, and, since I was able to reduce the company's overall expenditures from the start, I had a cushion of funds in place for any discrepancies. Most personal expenditures tend to be regular as well or can be forecast to provide reliable estimates. Simple expense charts are illustrated in the next chapter. They will help you to fine-tune cash control and estimate expenses by setting your own spending priorities. The following is an example of a Cash Flow Statement.

CASH FLOW STATEMENT

October 1st to December 31st				
Date	Description	Cash out	Cash in	Balance
Oct. 1	Balance forward			$1,000
Oct. 1	Mortgage	$325		
	Visa	225		
		$550		(550)
				$ 450
Oct. 7	Cash	$ 50		(50)
				$ 400
Oct. 15	Paycheque		$500	500
				$ 900
Oct. 18	Utilities	$150		(150)
				$ 750
Oct. 30	Paycheque		$500	500
				$ 1,250
Nov. 1	Balance forward			$ 1,250
Nov. 1	Mortgage	$325		
	Visa	125		
		$450		(450)
				$ 800
Nov. 3	Cash	$100		(100)
				$ 700

Date	Description	Cash out	Cash in	Balance
Nov. 15	Paycheque		$500	500 $1,200
Nov. 18	Utilities	$100		(100) $1,100
Nov. 30	Paycheque		$500	500 $1,600
Dec. 1	Balance forward			$1,600
Dec. 1	Mortgage	$ 325		(325) $1,275
Dec. 5	Cash	$ 75		(75) $1,200
Dec. 15	Paycheque		$500	500 $1,700
Dec. 18	Utilities	$ 100		(100) $1,600
Dec. 30	Paycheque		$500	500 $2,100
Dec. 30	GIC	$1,100		(1,100) $1,000

Although this example is oversimplified, this type of statement is easy to create because it's similar to a chequebook record. The difference is that you create it three months ahead of the last transaction, not as you go along. Once you become familiar with your regular spending by using the expense chart in the next chapter, you'll be able to forecast your future expenses with their corresponding due dates. Regular income payments and their dates will also be easy to project. If you're on commission, you'll still have an idea of your income to be received, but probably not for the full 90-day period. Regardless, you can estimate your upcoming expenses and the income required to cover them. Just having that information puts you in control.

Knowing where you currently stand financially by calculating a Balance Sheet and an Income and Expense Statement, and being able to estimate your near future with a Cash Flow Statement, provide the basis for making sound monetary decisions.

It isn't difficult to make these personal financial statements. I started using an Excel spreadsheet, entering my figures on the computer, but later I preferred printing the charts and recording the figures by hand since it was easier to compare the statements spread out on my desk. Either way, it isn't hard to do. It isn't particularly fun either. But it is important. Businesses need financial statements to show how well (or how poorly) they are performing and to pinpoint where financial problems lie. Personal and household financial management should be treated like a business. It's money, after all, that will provide your desired lifestyle, and money will accumulate through efficient cash management.

To begin, you need to know where you stand. If you don't know where you are, you could be going anywhere. If you don't know where your problems are, you can't correct them. And if you don't know what you need, you probably won't get it. Statements, although tedious, are the easiest way to find out. And once you make them for yourself, it'll be that much easier to read corporate financial statements when you have money to invest. Also, many people make estimates, expense reports, and budgets as part of their job duties. If you can create business statements for your employer, you can create personal ones for yourself. Do it now and get it over with.

By this point, you should have an idea of how you're doing financially. Take a good look at your statements and see if you are following the corresponding principles of my plan, but don't despair if your current money handling doesn't come close to the rules. Don't give in to automatic negative responses that stop you from following your dreams. Most likely, negative thinking will be your biggest obstacle in achieving financial freedom. Although I didn't find monetary goals particularly daunting, every time I was hired for a new job (and there were many) I thought I'd never be able to learn or do everything my position required. But at each workplace, there were kind, patient people who helped me out. I persevered, and they forgave my mistakes, provided I didn't repeat them. Even when I made an occasional error several years later at one workplace, a very considerate staff member would console me by joking, "That's okay, you're still brand new here." At another job, when I made a mistake and became so overwrought with worry, a coworker faced me squarely and said, "There really isn't very much in life that can't be fixed." When she said that, I recalled my grandparents soothing my childhood catastrophes with the words "Don't worry — we fix!" So, if you come up short in measuring yourself against my money-handling rules, those rules will simply become your goals, and my procedure will show you how to accomplish them. Knowing where you are, as well as your problem areas, is just your starting point. If you didn't have anything to correct, you'd be retired! And, if you reach only a few goals, your finances are still bound to improve substantially. So carry on with the next chapters on my procedure, and don't worry. We fix.

GET SMART

- Control money — don't let it control you.
- It's easier to control expenses than income.
- The act of saving is omnipotent.
- Savings are generated by keeping a high percentage of all sources of incoming money.
- Savings priorities are debt elimination and RRSP contributions.
- Delayed gratification means earn first, then spend.
- Jobs and spending habits must not hinder financial goals.
- Take moonlighting opportunities: learn and earn.
- Buy a home in a good area with a 25%–40% down payment.
- Build a substantial and diversified net worth.

CHAPTER NINE

KEEPING TRACK MEANS KEEPING MONEY

Now that you have a clear picture of your current financial standing, try a few quick calculations.

(1) Divide your rent or mortgage payment by your
     total net income. It should be about 30%.

(2) Add up your total savings deposited over the
     same period as your net income and divide
     savings by earnings. Ideally, you ought to be
     saving about 30% of your income (to retire
     debts or the mortgage or for asset accumulation).

(3) Total all remaining expenses, except rent or
     mortgage, and divide that number by your net
     income. It should be about 30%.

Note that these suggested percentages are related to how you
divide your net income, not your spending. These guidelines
stress the importance of keeping current costs of living (not

including debt payments or shelter) to 30% of net income (defined as gross income less deductions). Your focus should be to shrink those current costs in order to create the remaining 30% cash flow necessary for eliminating existing debts, creating an emergency fund, making extra mortgage payments or saving for a down payment on a home, contributing to your RRSP, and building wealth. That way, about 60% of your net income can be used to accomplish the two initial goals of getting rid of your debt and owning your own home. If you're an average consumer, though, the figure from number 3 above will be a much higher percentage, likely from unconscious, uneconomical spending and servicing your debt load.

The suggested percentages, however, are not unreasonable. They allow a 10% leeway, and, based on my research of family spending patterns over the past century, I think you should be able to apportion your income at approximately 30%, 30%, 30%. Looking at magazines and books from 1900 to 1926, I discovered a surprising pattern of average family spending of net income.

Housing:	30–35%
Food:	15–25%
Clothing:	10–15%
Savings:	15–20%

From 1950 to the end of the century, though, the percentages changed noticeably.

Housing:	20–25%
Food:	14–20%
Clothing:	6–8%
Savings:	1–8%

Since the 1950s, then, savings have been far lower, and a much greater proportion of money has been spent on other consumer products and services. In fact, decades of consumption outpacing income have resulted in troublesome consumer debt levels. Interestingly, this trend ties in with the fact that universal credit cards have only been around for about 50 years.

I've always been a strong opponent of debt. Living a debt-free lifestyle is simply the fastest way to acquire wealth on a modest salary. Think about it. If you end up spending so much more than the original purchase prices of goods in the form of interest payments, it will take you much longer to become financially independent. Those interest payments could have been used to buy assets that appreciate in value and boost your balance sheet. Instead, debts will weigh down the liabilities side and hinder the accumulation of net worth. And it's net worth that will be needed to finance your early retirement. So you must dismiss debt.

Without debt, you can enjoy a better standard of living because you'll have more money to spend any way you please instead of losing it to credit payments. The money you'd have paid in interest charges could even be used to buy some luxury goods. And while you're deciding how to spend the cash to enhance your lifestyle, you'll earn even more money from the return on the savings.

You can't be financially free if you're shackled with debt. Your net income gives you the opportunity for freedom, but it's a limited resource that you should use to look after your present and your future. If you're an average Canadian, though, a good part of it is still paying for your past. It's time to move forward now. Eliminate consumer debt and work toward owning a home free and clear. Then you can acquire other assets faster and retire earlier. Think of all the retirees you know who own their homes outright and have no other debts. They know freedom. They just didn't find it soon enough.

You need to live somewhere, and I think it's better to own than to rent and improve someone else's balance sheet. But I also think you must be free of the mortgage as soon as possible. Any kind of debt is a weighty encumbrance and the opposite of freedom. No matter what the economic conditions, you don't want to be beholden to a mortgagee. If housing prices plunge and you have to move, the loss you incur will be offset by the similarly reduced price of the next home you buy. If you don't move, how does the devaluation affect you? It doesn't. In a period of real estate devaluation, if I had a mortgage, I could be paying more than the house is worth as an asset or investment. But my home is not an investment; it's my environment, my shelter, my escape from the outside world. I don't depend on its cash return or income flow to live. That's what investments are for or, in the worst-case scenario, a *job*. Even without cash flow, I need a place to live, and if it's paid for, the taxes and other costs are far less than rent. In good economic times, the value of my home may soar, and I could take advantage of the increase by downsizing or moving elsewhere. If my home is paid for, I have more options. Regardless of the market value at any time, though, I'll have a place to live or an asset that can be converted into cash, one opportunity that a tenant will never have. You must buy an affordable home.

There are many excellent books on home buying, and this is where research comes in. My parents were in real estate, and I worked at two other real estate companies as well as at new-home sites, so that kind of background helped me immensely when I bought my homes. I asked a lot of questions, but I also bought a few books on home inspection and repair, and they became a valuable part of my library. Read all you can, go to Open Houses, consult with agents, talk to builders at their sites, or even work part time in a real estate office for an education in itself and put that income toward a down payment.

As well, make an appointment with a mortgage officer at your local lending institution. Get some referrals for real estate lawyers and compare their fees. When you find a house you want to make an offer on, I'd advise you to hire a home inspector either before or after making the offer. Doing it before writing an offer can save you time and grief by disqualifying a home with problems. Otherwise, ask your lawyer about including a clause in the offer making the purchase conditional upon a satisfactory home inspection. I've found that the home inspectors insurance companies use are extremely thorough, and I suggest calling your insurer for the name of the service it contracts.

Buy *something*. As soon as I had a full-time income and a

down payment, I bought an affordable condo in a good area — not the most prestigious area of the city but certainly a "good" one. About the same time, I knew a young couple who'd just married and wanted to buy a home but couldn't afford a house or a condominium. So they bought a trailer home in a retirement community and spruced it up while continuing to save for a house. A few years later, they sold the trailer at a profit and bought a starter home. Another friend of mine bought a small house and built up some equity over the years. When he lost his job, he couldn't afford the mortgage payment, so he sold the house, took his equity, and bought a co-op apartment as a cheaper, temporary measure. But well after he found steady employment again, he decided to save money and keep the apartment, and who knows? He might be in early retirement right now.

Buy a condo, a townhouse, a starter home, or even a trailer. Be careful, though, of property taxes, insurance, utilities, and any maintenance fees — they could add up to be higher than your mortgage payment. Consider all expenses before deciding on the type of housing you're going to buy. After carefully determining costs, including those for renovations (the home inspection is useful here), buy one of the most inexpensive homes available in the same area — not one that's priced at the high end. If one home is priced for less than another on the same street, and it compares well structurally but needs some TLC, I'd buy the cheaper one. Decorating and landscaping can be inexpensive improvements, and with a lower-priced home there is more room for it to appreciate in value compared with a home on the same street at the top end of the value range. Consider buying a home that lends itself to being partially rented out, and check the zoning regulations before you buy. Try to get a vendor take-back mortgage because vendors can be open to more favourable terms for you. Also look for any government programs or aid. At the very least, shop for mortgages to get the best rates and early payment features.

But you won't be able to buy any home if you have too much consumer debt. If that's your problem, first check out your options to consolidate loans into one package with a lower interest rate. And then stop using credit! Many people get better terms for past debts but then continue racking up more debt. Don't do it! Do you really think financial lenders are only trying to help your personal finances with consolidation loans? Marketers know that, if you're in the habit of using consumer credit and your burden is somewhat alleviated, you'll tend to use more credit to fill the newly created void. It's a variation of that Parkinson's Law: "work expands so as to fill the time available for its completion." See it as debt expands to fill the amount of credit allowed. Don't fall into that trap!

I know you've heard of drastic ways to stop using credit, such as cutting up your credit cards or freezing them in ice. It's inconvenient to use only cash, but if that's what it takes then that's what you'll have to do. Credit counselling services are another option. Try your local phone book's Yellow Pages or government listings for help.

I think the best solution to get out of the credit habit is to zero-in on expenses. By making an effort to reduce them, you'll collect a surplus to be applied against old debts. To help

MONTHLY EXPENSES

DEBTS $

BASICS	HOME	DETAIL	HEAT	DETAIL	HYDRO	DETAIL	WATER	DETAIL	PHONE	DETAIL
$	$		$		$		$		$	

NECESSITIES	FOOD	DETAIL	TRANSPORT	DETAIL	PERSONAL	DETAIL	HOUSEHOLD	DETAIL	INSURANCE	DETAIL
$	$		$		$		$		$	

VARIABLES	FURNISHINGS	DETAIL	GIFTS	DETAIL	CLOTHING	DETAIL	RECREATION	DETAIL	HOBBIES	DETAIL
$	$		$		$		$		$	

UNUSUAL	AMOUNT	DETAIL	NOTES
$	$		

TOTALS

BASICS	$
NECESSITIES	$
VARIABLES	$
UNUSUAL	$

GRAND TOTAL $

you, I've created three charts. Turn to the sample Monthly Expenses chart and quickly review it. You'll notice a shaded space in the top right-hand corner labelled "Debts" where you keep a total of all outstanding credit payments, except your mortgage. Debt payments are not included in monthly expenses because they represent past spending, and the total outstanding is shown at the top of the page as a reminder of your priority in paying it off by reducing current expenses. Mortgage or rent is not included because it is a separate 30% expenditure. These expenses reflect your actual costs of living over a month's time. There are four major categories: Basics, Necessities, Variables, and Unusual. I've broken down expenses this way to help you understand that all costs of living are not equal. They range from need to want to unexpected to rarely occurring costs. They are also divided according to how much control you have in lowering the amount spent in each category. And these categories make it easy to determine if you're spending too much on wants versus needs.

The Yearly Expenses chart provides a record of total monthly expenses for one year. It also includes both a percentage column to measure your yearly progress and the monthly average expense, which is useful for financial forecasting.

Now turn to the Net Income and Savings chart. This is a simple example of keeping track of income and savings, including debt reduction. It's also a way of measuring savings as a percentage of net income.

From Chapter 8, you'll know if your income isn't meeting your expenses. By using these charts, you'll be reminded of your goal of clearing outstanding debt and not taking on any

YEARLY EXPENSES

	YEAR TOTAL	AVERAGE	%	JAN	FEB	MAR	APR	MAY	JUN	JUL	AUG	SEP	OCT	NOV	DEC
GRAND TOTAL															
UNUSUAL															
VARIABLES															
NECESSITIES															
BASICS															
HOME															
HEAT															
HYDRO															
WATER															
PHONE															
FOOD															
TRANSPORT															
PERSONAL															
HOUSEHOLD															
INSURANCE															
FURNISHINGS															
GIFTS															
CLOTHING															
RECREATION															
HOBBIES															

NET INCOME & SAVINGS

INCOME	TOTAL	JAN	FEB	MAR	APR	MAY	JUN	JUL	AUG	SEP	OCT	NOV	DEC
SALARY 1													
SALARY 2													
RENTAL INCOME													
YEAR TOTAL													

SAVINGS	TOTAL	JAN	FEB	MAR	APR	MAY	JUN	JUL	AUG	SEP	OCT	NOV	DEC
DEBT REDUCTIONS													
CREDIT CARDS													
LOANS													
MORTGAGE													
CASH SAVINGS													
INVESTMENTS													
RRSP													
GIC's													
CSB's													
BONDS													
STOCKS													
FUND A													
FUND B													
FUND C													
YEAR TOTAL													

more debt, and you'll know your current cost of living. I don't believe in assigning dollar restrictions to the different categories, as in a budget, because doing that has never worked for me. I tend to spend money how I please, regardless of my best intentions. The only restriction I make is the total amount I have to spread among all the categories. I'll show you in Chapters 11–14 how to reduce expenses based on your priorities, not on deprivation, to afford more spending in other areas. My examples of cost cutting will probably appear extremely frugal, but to me they weren't, and that's the whole point. It doesn't matter where *I* cut costs, because after you analyse your expenses *you'll* be choosing how you save the money for paying down your debt.

To give you incentive in avoiding any new debt, I didn't include a space for it on your Monthly Expenses chart. I'm assuming you've resorted to counselling, you're using only cash, or you've found some other solution to keep yourself from racking up more debt. For those of you who've developed enough willpower to focus on the ultimate reward of financial freedom rather than the latest tempting bauble, I have another suggestion: use one no-fee credit card that has a reward system, and choose a very low credit limit. If you know you have a limited amount for all your monthly purchases, you have to keep track of them or risk the embarrassment of standing in a busy checkout line with a counter full of goods and not being able to buy them. You still have the convenience of a card, you still get reward points for nothing, and you are forced to become a conscious spender. I think taking responsibility for your purchases this way is better than using a direct payment card. Chances are, with a debit card, you'll arrange for overdraft protection, currently at about 21% interest, just in case you want to buy more than you can afford. And guess what? You will. Simply because you know you can. Instead, if you choose a credit card limit based on your income and expense history, you'll keep your spending under control when you buy only the things you've decided are priorities, and you should be able to pay off the balance every month without incurring interest charges.

If you are determined to change uneconomical consumer habits and can muster a little self-discipline, you can follow my simple method for daily money transactions using

(1) **one widely accepted, no-fee, reward program credit card;**
(2) **one no-fee cash machine card;**
(3) **bank accounts that allow free cheques and withdrawals;**
    and
(4) **one no-fee savings account with a high daily interest rate.**

You might think it's not possible to handle your daily money transactions with just those four, but it is, and it's easier than you think. Once you've done a 90-day Cash Flow Statement, you'll know what your cash and bill requirements are over the next three months. Here's how it actually works.

(1) **All income is deposited into the savings account.**

(2) **The cash requirement for each week is withdrawn once.**

(3) **Almost every purchase is made with the credit card.**

(4) **Bills are paid by transferring from savings to chequing.**

And here are the details.

(1) The savings account I use is with ING Direct, which has been paying four percent daily interest and has no service fees whatsoever. It's convenient for me to do my banking at any time, 24 hours a day, over the phone. Since it's branchless banking, I keep track of the balance, writing a tally on the most recent statement as transactions occur. When the next statement arrives in the mail, I check ING's figures with mine and bring the balance forward to continue the process on the new statement.

(2) My cash requirement is very small, so I usually withdraw money only twice a month for those purchases I can't use my credit card for. Since I don't ever have much cash with me, I don't spend what I don't have. ING offers a no-fee cash machine card.

(3) I use my Royal Bank Classic II Visa for every

expense I can. If you do the same, you'll stop
making "dollar dribbler" impulse buys, because
you'll feel ridiculous putting a $3.95 purchase
on a credit card, and, if you have a self-
imposed credit limit that's large enough only to
cover cost-of-living expenses, it would be worri-
some to charge anything extra. Yet you'll have
convenience using the card, you won't feel
deprived by not having one, and you'll have a
few weeks to earn interest on the cash you'll
use to pay the bill. As well, even though this
card has a yearly fee of $15, you'll receive one
percent of total purchases back in the form of
major store coupons, which have always more
than offset the fee for me. Other banks offer
similar deals: CIBC currently has a no-fee Visa
card with a cash rebate of .25% to 1% of total
yearly purchases, and this rebate is applied
against the December Visa statement balance.
Check out the offers: it only takes a few phone
calls. I applied for a no-fee American Express
Air Miles card once just to get free groceries.
Right after I used the card the first time, I
received enough points for a $20 gift certificate
from a large supermarket chain. After a few
more bonus offers on purchases I was planning
to make anyway, using my American Express
card instead of my Visa card, I ended up with
$100 in groceries. When the bonuses stopped, I

cancelled the card. Money for nothing.

(4) Although I can pay for most expenses with my Visa, I pay bills such as taxes and utilities by cheque or automatic withdrawal. This is where standard bank accounts come in. Again, by creating Cash Flow Statements, I know when I'll need to make bill payments and how many I'll have each month. I mark a calendar a few days ahead of each bill's due date. When the bills come in, I write the payment amounts on the calendar. Since I use my Visa for most expenses, I never have more than six bills to pay in any given month, so I opened six Royal Bank Calculator accounts. These are savings accounts with chequing privileges that allow one free cash withdrawal or cheque per month. I use the bank's free counter cheques, so my banking never costs me a cent. When a bill payment is due, I use the automated phone service at ING to transfer money into the Royal Bank account. Unfortunately, ING allows only three externally linked accounts, so for the other three accounts I have my GST rebate, tax refund, and small library paycheques deposited directly into them. On rare occasions, when I need all six accounts for withdrawals, I transfer money between some of them, but doing that still doesn't cost me anything. No service charges or fees. That's the way to do your banking.

Here's another reason to have only one credit card: it's easier to notice any fraudulent activity if you have only one card. And it doesn't have to be lost or stolen for the fraud to occur. It happened to me. I'd been using my Royal Bank Visa for years but decided to get a TD Visa for the convenience of cashing cheques at a nearby branch and for use in an emergency. It was a no-fee card, and I asked for a very low credit limit since I wouldn't be using it for purchases. I had the card for only a month when one Sunday afternoon I received a phone call from a TD Visa security officer. She said that they had to stop a transaction on my card a few hours before. I couldn't figure out what she was talking about. Then she said it was for an Internet purchase of $2,300. Not only had I never made a web buy, but also I had never used the card! I told her that *I* hadn't done it, and she conceded that there hadn't been any other card charges except for an $18 purchase, again on the web, a few days before. I asked her how someone could have got my card number and information, and she told me that personal information isn't needed on the Internet, just the card number. But how did someone get my Visa number? The card hadn't been in circulation at all. I didn't keep it in my purse since I didn't need it, and in fact I kept the card locked up with my other financial papers. I'd taken it out of the house once to cash a cheque at the bank, where only the teller had seen it. I'd never given the number out. How could this fraud have happened? The woman explained that it could have been a computer hacker. Then, a few months later, I called the security department to see if the criminal had been caught, and the man I spoke with said that it's entirely up to the retailer to follow up on such cases. I asked him how the thief had gotten my card number, and he said he didn't really think it was a hacker, but that was a "scary" possibility. He also admitted hesitantly that, since only I and TD Visa had the charge card number, it could have been an internal problem. He didn't have any other explanation. Regardless of how the fraud was done, there is an important lesson in this episode. You should always check every item on your credit card statement to ensure that no one else has made a purchase using your card.

Throughout the month, as I make purchases, I keep the receipts, and when I get home I put them away in my money binder, which includes the Monthly Expenses chart, Record of Banking sheet, and Cash Flow Statement. A few times a month, I record the expenses and then keep a running total of the credit card receipts, written on the back of the outermost slip. I keep these receipts together in a small plastic folder in the binder. After I record each cash purchase, I put the receipts in a series of "paid" envelopes according to the type of expense. When a credit card statement comes in, I match the receipts from the folder to it and check the statement entries for accuracy. I tally a new total on the back of the receipts that don't appear as charges and save them for next month's statement. Then I staple the matching receipts to the back of the current statement. For utility bills, I won't have any receipts to match against them, but I will need to record the overall amount on my Monthly Expenses chart. As already mentioned, I note the amounts and payment due dates on a calendar as well as the dates to transfer money from ING to my chequing/savings accounts. The payments will be either postdated cheques or automatic withdrawals. Cheques are mailed out with the dates circled in red. The bills stay in the binder until I actually transfer the money from ING and can mark them "paid" along with the dates (and the dates mailed in the case of postdated cheques). Then I put the bills in their individual "paid" envelopes. I keep all envelopes for that calendar year separately in a small box.

I recognize that couples may need to use some creativity in applying my money-handling system. Perhaps one person could use the charge card for household expenses and look after all the bill paying. The Cash Flow Statement will show how much each person needs for other daily expenses, which could be covered by the weekly cash withdrawal. One boss of mine used to receive a weekly allotment of cash from his wife for pocket money. When he spent it, there was no more. That system must have worked for them. I know that my parents plan their finances together and take turns paying the bills. Maybe that method keeps the lines of communication open and requires both parties to be responsible. If you have a partner, you both have to agree on your money-handling system. And if you begin by focusing on how much you need to spend (expenses) rather than on how much you have available to spend (income), you'll be off to a good start. Try the methods suggested in this chapter, or make some variations, but work them out together.

And while we're still talking about banking, be sure to

RECORD OF BANKING

Acct.#1	Detail	Acct.#2	Detail	Acct.#3	Detail	Acct.#4	Detail	Acct.#5	Detail	Acct.#6	Detail

check for any forgotten bank accounts that might still have some money on deposit. It's easiest to look for unclaimed accounts on the Internet at http://ucbswww.bank-banque-canada.ca.

Now, when you see your spending habits in chart form, you'll be able to scrutinize the expenses and determine where you need to make reductions. The next few chapters are filled with ideas on actually accomplishing that goal. Then, as your expenditures get smaller, you can use the surplus to establish an emergency fund, pay off previous debts (including your mortgage), and build capital for retirement.

In the meantime, you'll become so efficient at forecasting income and expenses, and handling daily cash requirements, that your use of bank accounts, cheques, and credit cards will be simplified. Really. It's just planning ahead and getting used to a system. I've included the Record of Banking sheet that I use for keeping track of my banking activity. It takes very little time to fill in while I'm banking on the phone. I'll bet you waste more time than you realize paying bills for various charge cards and other debts, and constantly running around to cash machines, never mind having an idea of the costs involved. As an experiment, add up all those little transaction fees and charges over an average month and multiply the figure by 12. Wouldn't you rather have spent that cash on something else? Simplify your money handling, save time in trips, and put money in *your* pocket instead of the bank's.

Try customizing the sample charts for your own circumstances — and then use them. Get into a routine. You'll be in control of your finances, and you'll have peace of mind.

You'll also have a clearer idea of your real costs of living in retirement. You already know that

1) income = expenses + savings (if any)

and that

2) expenses = debts (past purchases) + current costs.

Assuming that you aren't buying on credit anymore, your monthly expenses will reflect your cost of living or, put another way,

3) monthly income - debt payments - savings = cost of living.

Once you've reduced your monthly expenses using the ideas from the next four chapters, and once you've made a few forecasting adjustments, I think you'll have a much more accurate indication of your living costs in retirement than by using an "expert" formula based on current gross income. With debts out of the way, adjustments made for work-related expenses, and cost-of-living expenses reduced, you may be surprised at how little early retirement could actually cost. I was.

But there's no way around it — you have to do the math. Start by knowing where you stand right now.

FIRST THINGS FIRST

- Know where you stand financially.
- Get rid of old debts.
- Buy a home.
- Don't take on any new debt (except a mortgage).
- Recognize the potential loss from theft.
- Save money with lower-cost or free alternatives.

CHAPTER TEN

GET RICH NOW

Okay. You should have a good understanding of your current financial position. I imagine that the prospect of getting your current living expenses down to 30% of net income seems impossible. Maybe you think it can be done only if you have more money, but that kind of thinking is a major psychological roadblock. Another variation of Parkinson's Law from Chapter 8 needs to be mentioned here: spending expands so as to use up the amount of increased income. The more money you have coming in, the greater the temptation to increase your spending proportionately. Money magazines regularly feature examples of high-income couples living large on consumerism and teetering on the brink of financial ruin. Surely you know people who earn exceptional incomes yet can't seem to live within their means. Similarly, those in the "feast or famine" occupation of real estate sales acknowledge the tendency to fritter away money in good times and then regret not having saved for the inevitable bad times. A big income can lure you into a false sense of having big money to spend. Don't forget: we all have limitless wants and desires. So it's not the failure to earn more, it's the failure to spend less. But whatever your income level, be aware of what I refer to as your true disposable income: the amount you actually have available to spend after all deductions and employment-related expenses. This is the amount after all set costs related to generating the income are deducted, including taxes, other payroll deductions (e.g., union dues, health and pension plans), and any job costs. It's how I've always determined my true net funds: the amount left over to spend however I please. As a formula, it's stated as

gross income - compulsory income-related expenses
= true disposable income.

It's not how much you're getting, it's what you have left over after deducting the costs of getting it. How you use those funds will give you a better idea of retirement expenses since you're excluding current employment-related costs, which will likely disappear in retirement. And it's not how much you have left over, it's what you do with what you have left over that ultimately creates the wealth for retirement.

Perhaps it's a different perspective, but I think you need to regard your disposable income as the net profit from your business of working. If you ran a business, your profit would be gross receipts (all money coming in) less business expenses (all costs related to the business). You really should see your personal income the same way. Doing that helps you to pinpoint your actual spending potential for all your other needs and wants, such as debt elimination, home purchase and/or mortgage discharge, costs of living, savings, and luxuries.

Your true disposable income, then, might be quite a disappointment in relation to your gross income. But whatever it is, that's the amount you have to work with in amassing capital for your early retirement.

To achieve the goals of clearing debts and buying a home, you could try increasing your income, and I recommend multiple streams of income for accelerating your early retirement date, but it will take time, effort, and possibly additional work-related costs. Better still to shrink expenses first. You don't have much control over your income, but you have complete control over your cost-of-living expenses. I've found that it takes less time and effort to reduce expenses than to increase income. You'll learn how to live within your means, free up cash to eliminate debts and add assets, and splurge on your priority luxuries.

Nobody likes the idea of cutting back. Deprivation is an ugly word. So is poverty. But it doesn't have to be that way. If you're cutting back from overconsumption, you won't be lacking; you'll have less, but only compared with too much. Since there's no end to your wants, there's also no end to the list of things you don't need. There is a limit, however, to what you need to survive, to be healthy, comfortable, and content. My definition of freedom doesn't equal an infinite amount of money. It isn't a set number printed in a bankbook or on a balance sheet. It's being rich enough to independently cover all your needs and have enough left over to afford security, comfort, and the fulfilment of your most important desires. So being "rich" is having enough to finance the freedom to pursue your dreams. And you can become richer right now by lowering your expenses.

If you know your disposable income and your regular expenses, you're in a position of power — you can take control. You can decide how a limited amount of money is going to be spent. And, by keeping the goal of financial freedom foremost in your mind, you can then decide how to lower your expenses.

Apportion your money by determining your own priorities for cost-of-living expenses. Just knowing how you currently spend your money can help you to decrease some costs. It's the concept of value versus time and effort. After filling in your Monthly Expenses chart, you may have been surprised at how much you actually spend on certain items over a month's time. It was probably easy to recognize that you weren't getting value for your money in some areas. "Hard-earned money" means just that: the time and effort you had to *spend* in exchange for income. When you spend money, you're really spending part of your limited time here on Earth and some degree of effort. The product or service you received in return — was it worth it? Take a good look. Do you think you should have given up less of your life for it? That's what cutting expenses is all about. Not becoming poor or deprived but getting your life back.

Whenever you spend money, you should compare what you have to do with what you really get; you should be aware of how much time and effort are required to get the disposable income to pay for it. But be careful! You might judge your time to be worth more than it actually is. Say, for example, you consider your time to be worth more than a house cleaner's because you earn $25 per hour and pay only $10 per hour for the service. Even if you make $25 an hour after taxes and all work-related costs have been deducted, your hourly worth is still limited by the total number of hours in a day that you can actually work. That set income can cover only so many expenses, and, if it's already paying for everything else, essentially you have to work additional hours, assuming that's even possible, to pay for the cleaner. And do you really want to work *more?*

Look at it this way: say you can earn only $1,000 per month of disposable income and your current monthly expenses are also $1,000. You can't afford the additional cost of a cleaner, no matter how little you have to pay, unless you give up some other current expenditure. In effect, you'd have to make a trade-off by deciding whether having someone else clean your house is more important to you than some other existing need or want. You have to look at all your costs of living and make a decision based on your priorities.

Paying taxes and bank service charges, and being swayed into paying more for a standard or joyless product, are my most hated expenses. So I've tried to legally avoid, reduce, or get rid of these costs. In the previous chapter, I discussed how I eliminated bank charges and earn the highest rate of return available instead. Avoiding taxes is another challenge.

Taxes are a huge cost of living relative to personal time and effort required to earn the income to pay for them. Hidden taxes, property taxes, GST, provincial sales taxes, payroll taxes, and income taxes effectively lower your current standard of living. As long as you need your job for a source of income to pay for past debts and current and future costs, you have little control over those taxes. My efficiency in handling expenses and my lack of debt have resulted in a cost of living that requires only a small income, which the government deems unworthy of taxation. Whenever my income exceeds the basic personal amount on my annual tax return, I'm able to reduce my taxable income to zero by deducting only enough of my RRSP contributions to fall below the tax-exemption line. The balance of my contributions I carry forward to use in any year when my taxable income rises. As well, because of my low income level, I'm not worthy of being taxed fully on my property or purchases, so I receive yearly rebates for municipal, Ontario, and GST taxes.

If I chose to pay for all the services I can do myself, I'd have to spend more time and effort working to earn the money to share with the tax man and the hired service. The tax grab hits me coming and going. So instead of working at a "job," I work at the services and make the products that I would have needed the income for. Either way takes time and effort, but I choose the nontaxable way. Since taxes are charged on buying and earning, I avoid buying and earning. Taxes aren't charged on food for making meals at home, or on borrowing materials from the library, or on doing my own landscaping. It takes me 15 minutes to shovel the snow on my driveway and sidewalk. A neighbourhood service charges $20, and I can't justify paying $80 per hour on something that I can easily do.

If I was in a 40% tax bracket, I'd need to earn $134 to pay for something that takes 15 minutes a week over a month. But since I'm not wasting my time at a taxed job, I have time to work at those formerly taxable services and to make those previously taxable products.

I have to buy some things, of course, but again I choose the lowest price or a nontaxable method: buying consciously, buying value, buying at a discount, buying alternatives, or buying used. I can't understand why anyone would pay $8–$10 for a bottle of shampoo or "styling product" that has the same proportion of identical ingredients as one for two dollars. The same goes for cosmetics. A very helpful book in proving this fallacy of product differentiation is *Don't Go to the Cosmetics Counter without Me*, by Paula Begoun. Not only are many products the same, but also they are made by the same manufacturer.

The "more is better" theme of consumerism also holds little appeal for me. Surprisingly, I've found quality over quantity to be cheaper as well. Since the higher-value purchase returns a higher degree of satisfaction, I don't tire of my purchase, look for the "new and improved" model, or want to buy different and more objects to compensate for the lack of pleasure that a lower-value purchase gives. The satisfaction from taking the Concorde to France far surpassed the enjoyment I would have had from a few insignificant trips of total equal value. One beautiful antique piece of jewellery with an intriguing history gives me more pleasure than a couple of new pieces of "good" jewellery or a box full of pricey costume jewellery. One soft suede shirt feels so much nicer on the skin than half a dozen scratchy synthetic tops. You get the idea.

Quality over quantity also solves the problem of accumulating clutter. My grandmother used to refer to it as "junk and garbage." I champion the trend to declutter because it provides a good incentive to rank consumer products. Simplicity is currently in style, and, if it makes it easier to clear out the junk, so much the better. But don't fall into the automatic consumer response of replacing all the old discarded goods with new stuff! Remember Parkinson's Law, which in this case would be "clutter expands so as to use up the amount of increased space." I know someone who used to follow that fill-it-back-up-again routine. She'd do a major clean-out and then go on a spending spree to replace the various objects. She'd stage regular acts of clearing out the clutter, and then replenishing it, until it got too expensive. Even then she didn't stop; she bought items at discount stores, then charity shops, and finally garage sales. The buy-purge-buy-purge cycle was a habit. Fortunately, she finally changed this financially destructive behaviour, shunning the "more is better" belief and adopting the "best is best" approach. Now her home is a calming retreat filled with her carefully chosen favourite furnishings. That's conscious spending.

Rediscover your own favourite things. Move furniture around, including mirrors and pictures, and reaffirm why you bought them. If the reasons don't seem very good now, or you can't figure out why you bought the items, get rid of them. But try to get some cash first: place a free ad on a local bulletin board, in a newspaper, or over the radio; ask friends or coworkers if they know anyone who's looking for whatever you're selling; hold a garage sale (better yet, a street sale and split the ad cost); or give the stuff to a charity that issues tax receipts for donations. A word about garage sales, though. Their popularity seems to have diminished lately, but last year the street sales in my city attracted more people. Best of all was an estate garage sale that I had to sell the rest of my aunt's belongings, along with some of my own things, my parents', and my friend's. I held it with my friend at my parents' house, which is considered to be in an "upper crust" area. On the morning of the sale, so many people arrived that the road became choked with traffic, and my poor friend had to fight through the throng on foot all the way from the end of the street. People couldn't shove their money at us fast enough, and our inventory was quickly cleaned out. We both felt overwhelmed and tired — but not too tired to count our money.

If you don't think you'll be able to sell your castoffs, think again. Your style of consumption is always relative to someone else's. A few years ago, I had an old dot-matrix printer that a friend had given to me. It was perfectly fine for my use — and free! Then, when my brother updated his computer system, he gave me a better printer, so I placed a free ad in the newspaper to sell the old dot-matrix. I didn't expect to get any calls, but it didn't cost anything to try. As it turned out, I had one response. A man came to my house, paid $20, and was happy to have the printer for his teenage daughter. All you need, after all, is just one buyer.

So go through everything for a good clear-out, make some money, and then resist the temptation to buy anything more. Take the time to try living without so many things — after a few months, you probably won't miss anything anyway, but if you do you'll know it's a priority. Take the plastic off your rugs, sofa arms, and lampshades, use your "company" linens and your best housewares, and wear your nicest clothes. When my aunt passed away, my mother inherited cedar chests full of fine linens and bedding that my aunt had been saving for "good." Good might never come. Indulge in your best now. And these furnishings don't have to be your most expensive; they can be possessions that have real sentimental value or simply make you happy. Sell or give away the rest, including gifts you've received but never really liked. Give yourself permission to ignore your guilt and get rid of them. It was the feeling offered with the present, not the present itself, that was the real gift. Go through your basement, storage locker, garage, and attic too. A friend of mine has made about $400 each year from the past three annual "used kids' stuff" community sales. Another friend takes her castoffs to resale and consignment shops. There are used-goods stores that buy everything from clothing and jewellery to sports equipment and appliances. I've taken my clothing and accessories (even shoes) to consignment shops many times. Some store owners will give you cash outright, and others will offer a percentage of the eventual selling prices of your goods. If you have many large items to go, invite a local auctioneer over for advice. You may be able to combine your lot with others in an upcoming sale. Whatever you decide, clear the clutter, get some cash, and resist the temptation to buy replacements.

Now that only your finest and most favourite things make up your environment, you should feel richer. You certainly shouldn't feel deprived. And, if you've made some cash, you are richer. Your home and closets should look bigger too.

With fewer worldly goods, you'll waste less time and money on maintenance. Just think of what you could miss: replacement costs, repairs, insurance, licence fees, upgrading, cleaning, storing, and carting around. Less clutter means more time to enjoy the things you do have, just like retirees do.

Reduced buying also means that you'll have fewer items to record on your Monthly Expenses chart and possibly fewer bills to pay.

When you're contemplating which expenses to eliminate, watch for the trap of assuming that low-priced items don't affect your priorities. One probably doesn't, but the combination of many low-priced products may chisel away at your savings potential. Why are dollar stores so profitable? Because of sheer volume. It's easy for people to spend a few dollars here and there, even on junk, because it doesn't seem to be a big waste of money. That is, not until you calculate the whole amount you've spent on insignificant purchases over a month or a year. And think about how many times you use this mindset for coffee and a doughnut, a newspaper or magazine, cable channels, public television membership, telephone add-on service, disposable anything — they all seem to cost too little per day to care about. But if you make multiple low-priced purchases *every* day, can you see how quickly they'd add up over a year? After totalling a year of the coffee-doughnut-newspaper expense, you'll realize that you could have spent the money on a very good dishwasher instead. You won't have to do without. Find alternatives. The news is on the radio and TV, daily newspapers are at the library, most workplaces have a coffeemaker, and your heart or waistline probably doesn't need the doughnut. Over time, these aren't insignificant expenses, and, if you don't have money for luxuries, that could be why.

Likewise, the "combination" concept shows how you can accelerate savings. The money you save by not buying little items repeatedly adds up just as quickly over a month or a year as your "dollar dribblers" do. Combined savings generated by completely cutting out some costs and reducing others will provide a decent sum to be applied against old debts and the mortgage or to be added to your capital base. It's money for luxuries too.

Even on my meagre disposable income, I was able to channel most of it into mortgage reduction and savings, but regularly I indulged in some big luxury item without buying it on credit. The cash came from the reduced cost-of-living expenses.

There are so many ways to decrease costs. Some books offer reams of lists on how to pinch pennies. I get bored reading those books with chapter after chapter of miserly tips, many of which don't relate to my lifestyle. I think it's far better to offer suggestions on how you approach consumption. The act of consuming, whether goods or services, is really your cost of living. Therefore, understanding and adopting the most economical mind-set toward consumption will result in the most economical cost of living. That means rejecting marketing ploys and media-influenced cultural standards and deciding for yourself what's most important in life. It means owning rather than renting, avoiding taxes, living debt free, and becoming more self-sufficient. It also means buying less.

To decrease expenses, you need to buy fewer things and

spend less on the remaining items. Quality over quantity. Conscious spending. Priority purchases. Value in return for time and effort spent. Do it yourself. And reduce, renew, reuse.

If you've reduced the clutter in your home, you'll be aware of the potential for reducing purchases. You didn't really need or want all that stuff you bought and have now gotten rid of. They couldn't have been priority buys in the first place. So, before you buy anything else, ask yourself, "Do I really *need* this? Will it help me to pay off my old debts? Will it bring financial freedom closer?" No? Then don't buy it. Nobody's forcing you. It's a simple choice. Know your priorities.

But suppose you stop the impulse there, and then, over the next few weeks, you keep thinking about how much you want it. That item has now become a priority luxury to save for. Remember delayed gratification? Delaying a purchase is disappointing, but it's gratifying to look forward to buying the item, to have a sense of accomplishment when you buy it for cash, and to feel smug since you know that most people end up paying far more than the sticker price because they use credit. While they keep making interest payments for past purchases, you'll have money for current buys or to help secure your future. And there's another bonus. Instead of paying the bank to buy something (interest charges), let the bank pay *you* with a return on your savings (interest income). That way, you pay less than the product's purchase price every time. Don't forget, too, that prices generally come down over time, so an item might be cheaper by the time you have the cash to buy it.

"Don't throw it out!" was a familiar refrain during my childhood. It was usually followed by "That's still *good!*" I think my mother was influenced the most by her parents, who never wasted anything in their household. My grandparents lived through the Depression, but they were thrifty by nature. They raised chickens to provide eggs, meat, and soup for their family and to sell the extra eggs. Feathers were tied around a scrap piece of wooden dowel to use as a duster, and the down was saved for stuffing cushions. But their use of the chicken didn't end there. They had an old wood cookstove, and the charred remains from the fire had to be regularly cleaned out. My grandmother used an old metal pan to catch the ashes and a dried chicken wing, white feathers intact, to brush out the stove. It was a little unnerving to see a chicken wing lying in the dustpan. However, it did seem to be designed for easy sweeping action, where the top bone made a well-fitting grip between thumb and forefinger.

Now I've never recycled animal parts, but I reuse products whenever I can. Once you reduce your belongings, your remaining goods take on greater value and should be looked at closely before they're thrown away. When clothing styles changed, I took the shoulder pads out of blouses, cut off the fabric, and used the foam to store breakables. I also cut the foam into circles and triangles to be used as cosmetic puffs and rectangles to be used as cleaning sponges. I thought of these uses because I would have bought the foam products anyway. As I removed the shoulder pads, my thought process went like this: "Don't throw it out! What is this really in its most basic form? Foam. Padding. What do I spend money on that is basically the same thing? Sponges. Puffs. Cushioned wrap." It's looking at a basic material for what it is, not what it's sold as. On a few occasions, I've caught my mother holding some article about to be discarded and staring into space, consumed by the task of thinking of another use for the article. But it's worthwhile only if you need it and can use it. Otherwise, it's just junk.

The important thing is how you look at throwaways — a lampshade with a ripped covering is really just a wire form. I need wire forms for my garden, so it becomes a tomato cage or other plant prop that I won't need to buy.

Renewing is another way to cut down on purchases. After a few years, my brass mailbox lost its sheen and turned an unattractive colour. I didn't need to buy a new one — it still held my mail — I just needed a better-looking one. So I polished and urethaned the old one, and it was as good as new for a few more years. Then, when it eventually turned dull, I spray painted the lid gold and the rest glossy black with an outdoor paint. The urethane and paints were leftovers from other jobs, so instead of buying two new mailboxes I renewed the original one, twice, for free.

The same thought process should be used in any buying decision, whether for needs or for wants. It is especially economical when purchasing items that you need for living but that offer little joy in return. Take, for example, food storage containers. What are they in their most basic form? Zipper bags that change colour when zipped? No, simply plastic bags. Are they decorator-coloured plastic boxes? No, just plastic containers with lids. Then the next question is "Where can I get them free?" Recycled milk bags are great for storing frozen food and are kept closed with plastic bread bag ties, grocery bag ties, or elastic bands (my mailman has an annoying habit of leaving rubber bands on my porch, but at least they're free). Stretch plastic, foam trays, and plastic containers and jugs find many new uses in and around my house. Food storage, seedling pots, watering cans, and insulation all come from product packages. I throw foam meat trays into my attic for extra insulation, and some I've cut to fit behind outlet and switch plates to stop air leaks. In hardware stores, these foam draft protectors are called "gaskets." They're just thin styrofoam, free from your supermarket's produce and meat departments. You can find so many little items for free if you just look at them for what they really are or do. For example, I thought I needed to buy a hairband to keep my long hair back when washing my face. A purchase like that, even though small, would mean going to and from the store, being tempted to make other impulse buys while there, and paying taxes — all for a product that would give me little joy. What a waste of time, money, and effort! All I really needed was some stretchy fabric to pull my hair off my face. A ruined pair of pantyhose that I had saved to tie garden plants to stakes was perfect for this new use. It took less than two minutes to cut a piece, measure it around my head, and tie the ends. Instant hairband. Fast, easy, free.

For all potential purchases, I determine first if I want something badly enough to spend my limited amounts of time, effort, and money to get it. The question is, do I really need and want it? If so, I try to get it free by using something else, repairing it or making it myself from any materials on hand, or borrowing it. If it's a service rather than a product, I consider whether I can do without it, do it myself, have someone help me, or learn how to do it free of charge (volunteering, on-the-job training, library self-help materials, free seminars). If you need or want to buy something, try to get it free first.

Suppose you can't get it free. You're going to have to spend some money, but think of the alternatives beforehand. If, say, you need your carpets cleaned, you could pay for a service, buy a new or used cleaning machine, or rent one to do the work yourself. Think of all your options before parting with your cash.

The order of your buying options should be as follows.

(1) **Get it free.**
(2) **Borrow it or get someone to help you.**
(3) **Consider renting it by calculating cost versus amount of use.**
(4) **Buy it used at a discount (private sales, charity shops).**
(5) **Buy it used from a retailer.**
(6) **Buy it new at a discount (private, liquidator, surplus, on sale).**

Your last resort should be to buy a product new at a full-price retailer, but even then remember to buy only the basic product and no extras. Try, though, to get extras thrown in with your purchase. At a men's clothing shop, I watched a man get a free tie with his purchase when he asked for it. At one large department store, you'll get the hangers when you buy clothes. Ask.

One caveat about buying items used. At one time, I knew

a phone installer at Bell Canada, and whenever he removed a telephone from a house he had to seal it in a bag for fumigation back at the plant. I'm always concerned about bringing home more than I bargained for when I buy something used, so just to be safe I take the following precautions.

- ↦ In cold and flu season, believe it or not, I rub alcohol over the plastic covers on any borrowed materials from the library before I use them.
- ↦ Before I put any antique books in my library, I leave them outside, open to the sunshine to kill any mould spores, and then put them in my freezer for a month to kill any creepy crawlers.
- ↦ I wash used clothing and other items in hot or boiling water, or have them dry-cleaned, before I wear them.
- ↦ I've also used the Bell method, bagging objects, spraying the insides of the bags with bug killer, and keeping them tightly closed for a few days.
- ↦ I clean and disinfect any used article before bringing it inside my house.

My father told me a story recently about an inexpensive used bed that my grandfather bought during the 1930s. He and my grandmother had already bought a new mattress, but it was the old-fashioned used frame and springs that concerned her. When my grandfather brought the bed home to their farmhouse, she wouldn't allow it inside until she was convinced it wasn't carrying bedbugs. So she took the steel bedstead into a clearing, wrapped a rag around a pole, doused it in kerosene, set it ablaze, and torched the bed, effectively cremating any critter hiding inside. After the springs cooled down, she washed the soot off the blackened steel and finally allowed my grandfather to carry it into the house.

I realize that the examples given in this book are of exceptional economy, but they're used to illustrate a point. Please understand the distinction that extreme frugality is only for expenses that generate very little happiness. Savings on boring incidentals and unpleasant but necessary costs will provide you with the cash for eliminating debts and spending on goods and services that bring joy. The surplus adds to assets for freedom and allows luxuries for motivation. So decide what you hate spending money on, or which expenses give minuscule benefits to your lifestyle, and cut them to the quick. It's a way of apportioning your limited disposable income so there's more money for what you consider to be your more important wants. Then, although the luxuries may be expensive, they'll be affordable because you can buy each one in order of preference, pay for them with cash, and need fewer of them to be happy. That's why I don't believe in small luxuries. For me, regular little pleasures mean a life of mediocrity. I see it as settling for less. It's just not enough, and it doesn't even provide motivation to achieve my more substantial goals. I need extreme rewards to accomplish extreme success. Small treats make small impressions, and regular rewards quickly lose their impact. The more often you indulge, the more mundane it becomes. How can you appreciate something that you have all the time? Gifts that are enjoyed the most are those that occur the least often. It's best to have big luxuries — but not too often. They're affordable when you cut back on low-value purchases. Once you can differentiate your expenses by determining the value each provides (happiness quotient and route to freedom), you'll find it easier to reduce the unimportant ones by using the buying decision process.

The next four chapters offer suggestions on how to apply your new purchasing behaviour to all of your current costs of living. You'll have noticed on the Monthly Expenses chart that they're divided into Basics, Necessities, Variables, and Unusual. I've separated expenditures this way because doing that focuses on their capacity for being reduced. Basics are more fixed in their costs than Variables — property taxes are more difficult to reduce than entertainment spending. Knowing this will make it easier for you to achieve higher savings in some areas. If you can't save much on one expense, don't be discouraged, because you can simply decide to save more money in another category where there's a better opportunity for you to do so. Remember that the Monthly Expenses chart doesn't reflect all your monthly outlays. Its purpose is to help you focus on reducing current cost-of-living expenses to an ideal 30% of your net income so that your debts and mortgage will benefit from the cuts. If you're still paying rent, that expense should be exchanged for a monthly mortgage payment as soon as possible. Any remaining debt total is shown, every month in the top right-hand corner of the chart, as a reminder of why you're cutting costs.

Breaking it all down this way makes money management

so much easier. You decide where and how much to eliminate or cut back. You have complete control.

FINE-TUNE CASH FLOW

- Sell your clutter.
- Enjoy what you have.
- Seek alternatives to buying.
- Prioritize spending.
- Purchase value.
- Spend consciously.
- Consider buying used.
- Take control of all your expenses.

CHAPTER ELEVEN

THE CHALLENGE:

BASICS

B asic expenses are costs that are essential for living and the most difficult to reduce. In the case of my own finances, these costs are for Home, Heat, Hydro, Water, and Phone. Each one is fairly set, already at the lowest possible rate, and it would take a considerable change in my lifestyle to reduce them further.

My expense heading for "Home" includes only property taxes. As explained in the previous chapter, the Monthly Expenses chart excludes rent or mortgage payments and other debt repayments since the only reason for scrutinizing the remaining costs of living is to provide cash savings to alleviate those debts and build assets. When you are able to lower current costs to about 30% of net income, a home becomes affordable with a monthly mortgage payment of about 30%, and another 30% can be used to eliminate liabilities and/or increase savings for early retirement. The remaining 10% provides a cushion for miscalculations. Then, when you reach early retirement the same way I have, there won't be rent or mortgage payments at all.

Other than changing your place of residence, you have very little control over property taxes. You can do some research to see if your property appears to be unfairly assessed and make an appeal though. In Ontario, contact the Assessment Review Board at 1-800-263-3237 or visit the web site at www.arb.gov.on.ca for details. In other provinces, check the government phone listings for the equivalent board and the public municipal tax rolls that give your area's property assessments. There may also be a government-funded local assessment office that offers more information on comparable properties. Or you can call a real estate appraiser for advice or even hire one to file an appeal for you. If, on the other hand, you choose to file it yourself, your local board will send out the necessary forms. When I last checked, it cost $50 to file an appeal in Ontario.

Years ago, I could get a discount for sending my property taxes in early, and the deduction was higher than any rate of return (less income tax) that I could have received on the money as savings. It could be an option for you, depending on where you live. But since the discount isn't available in my city anymore, I never pay my property taxes in advance, and I can't understand why anyone would. Instead of paying your taxes ahead of time (which includes choosing the option of monthly payments over quarterly bills), you can earn a return on your funds before the rest of the taxes are due.

The next category is home heating. It's definitely a basic cost-of-living expense, high on the scale of needs. My house is heated by oil, and, based on my history of moving fairly often, I couldn't justify the expense of changing the whole heating system over to gas, including a new higher-efficiency furnace. But there are a number of small ways I save on heating costs. The furnace is regularly cleaned, and the temperature settings on the fan controller were changed so that the fan starts blowing the hot air through the ducts sooner and shuts off at a lower temperature. I have an electronic air cleaner, and I make sure it's kept clean. If your furnace has a standard filter, buy the kind you can clean yourself. Disposable ones get expensive. I also bought a programmable thermostat that automatically turns the heat on 15 minutes before I get up in the morning and lowers it about two hours before I go to bed. A long-standing joke in our family is that each of us thinks the other members keep their houses too cold. When I was growing up, my mother used to tell me to "Put a sweater on!" I suppose it's what you get used to, because now I keep my thermostat set at 20°Celsius (68° Fahrenheit) during the day and 15°Celsius (58° Fahrenheit) at night. My relatives regulate their heat similarly. The funny thing is, whenever we visit each other, we bundle up in our warmest clothes before going over, thinking that we'd better prepare for the miserly heat conservation, while the relative there hastily turns up the thermostat so as not to look cheap. Then, as we arrive, we can't believe how hot the house is and spend the visit looking forward to returning to our own, cooler houses.

I'm not cold in my house because I dress for the seasons, and in winter I have a warm down-filled duvet for sleeping. I like the home decor style of blinds and heavy drapes, which help to insulate against summer heat and winter cold. The blinds cost about two dollars each at Wal-Mart. I don't remember if I checked for lead content in the PVC, but I don't plan to be licking my blinds. The nonstandard-sized ones were priced higher, but the ones for two dollars were good enough for my windows. Where they were too big, I simply trimmed the slats and cut the header down. My hacksaw has served me well over the years.

I've already mentioned reusing foam meat trays for gaskets behind electrical plates on outside walls and putting scrap styrofoam in the attic. Insulate your home if possible, but at least seal any drafts.

I discovered that I don't need to heat the upstairs during the day, and, since heat rises, by nightfall it's warm up there, and I only need to open the registers for heat overnight and for first thing in the morning. When I leave the house, I turn the thermostat down to 15°, and when I return the fuel oil burns so hot that the house heats up quickly. Try lowering your heat a few degrees. The lower temperature might make you feel less sluggish during the day and help you to sleep better at night. I *like* it cooler now. But I still have to remember to turn the heat up when regular folk come to visit.

I also call around for the best oil delivery price. When a tank is being filled with 900 litres, a few cents less a litre make it worthwhile. And I make sure that the oil company accepts Visa since I'll get one percent of the expense back. Remember, it's the combination of little incidental savings in many areas, done repeatedly, that really add up.

"Hydro" is an expense that I've had difficulty decreasing.

One success, though, was with my hot-water tank. When I moved to this house, there was an older electric water tank on rental. Being a firm believer in owning, not renting, I told a hydro representative that I was considering switching to gas and that he could come and get the rental. He said it wasn't worth the company's time to come and pick it up, so I got a free hot-water tank. The thermostat was set too high (I don't need scalding water out of every tap), so I lowered the temperature. My dishwasher has its own heater to thoroughly clean the dishes. And there's no sense in heating the whole water tank to wash a few delicate dishes by hand. I simply boil a measuring cup of water in the microwave and add it to the hot water in the sink.

For the hot-water tank to heat up more efficiently (and economically), I had to drain it. By doing that, the sediment resting on the coils washed out, leaving the bottom coil free to heat the water. Gas hot-water tanks should be periodically drained as well. Then I bought an insulating blanket for the tank and inexpensive foam pipe insulation for the hot-water supply lines. I also had a timer installed to heat the water only when I need it hot, usually an hour before I get up in the morning and an hour before supper. With the tank insulation, the water doesn't even need to be heated every day in the summer to maintain a hot temperature. And when I'm going to be away for a few days, I turn the heater off at the electrical panel. Be aware, though, that it's very dangerous to use an insulating blanket on a gas hot-water tank, and it's never advised. Unfortunately, you can't use a timer on a gas-heated water tank either.

Also, from June to September, I defrost my chest freezer and leave it turned off with the lid propped open so it doesn't smell. By the summer, I'm eating fresh foods mostly, and my refrigerator freezer is all I need for any frozen food. While the big freezer is unplugged, I save money on my hydro bill. Don't use hydro if you don't need it. Not surprisingly, I turn lights off in unused rooms. I'm amazed at the number of people who leave their televisions, computers, and stereo systems on when they're not in use. That's a lost opportunity to add to savings. It takes minuscule effort: push the buttons and turn them off.

Anything that uses electricity to produce heat is going to cost more, so use the most efficient ways possible. I needed one of those umbrella-style clotheslines, and my mother found one at a garage sale for a few dollars. I had a new driveway and patio under construction at the time, so I asked the contractor to lay some gravel in a back corner of my yard and set the clothesline in concrete for me. I knew it would be a bit of an eyesore, so I landscaped tall cedars in a curve in front of it, effectively blocking it from view. From April to November, I hang my laundry outside instead of using the dryer.

An ancient clothes dryer came with the house, and over the past eight years it's served its purpose for the winter months. There isn't much choice in settings, and it doesn't get really hot, but I only need it to dry, not bake, my clothes. I still take them out when they're damp and let them air-dry on the basement clotheslines. Since I use the dryer only in the coldest months, the furnace is usually on and radiates heat to help the clothes dry faster. Don't forget to look at a purchase in terms of how it serves your needs. I need a dryer to dry clothes. Period. The appliance doesn't fill me with joy, so I wouldn't spend a lot of money to buy one. I need dependability, but the dryer is in the basement, so a "scratch and dent" basic model would be just fine. And I'd enjoy spending on luxuries the hundreds of dollars that I'd save by buying a cheap dryer.

One costly small appliance is an iron, so do all your ironing at the same time or, like me, don't have very many clothes that need ironing. As far as other heat-generating appliances go, I prefer using my microwave because it's faster and easier than using my stove, and it's cheaper. When I do use the oven, it's to cook and bake a number of dishes at once.

Central air conditioning uses a lot of electricity as well. For years, I had trouble cooling the second floor of the house. Even though there was new duct work, insulation, extra roof vents, and an exhaust fan installed upstairs, I couldn't get an even temperature on both floors. I have a dark roof and sunny southern exposure, so the whole upstairs bakes. I added an awning to the front window and kept styrofoam over the ensuite skylight during the day, and they helped a little. Even then, if I turned up the central air conditioning enough for cool sleeping, the downstairs would be a cold-storage temperature all night for nothing. Big waste of money. So I resorted to buying an energy-efficient room air conditioner just for the upstairs bedroom. Now I hardly use the central air, and the room unit uses less electricity. The most important thing, of course, is my comfort, and in this case the solution happens to be cheaper. Yes, I bought an air conditioner, but, unlike the previous homeowner who had the central air installed, I'll keep the portable unit when I move. Remember assets with inherent value? And the reduction in my hydro bill offsets the cost of that purchase with every passing year.

"Water" is another basic but low-joy purchase. Since I'm billed for the amount of water I use in my home, I cut the cost by reusing it whenever possible. When I do laundry, I save both the wash and the rinse water in the laundry tubs. The sudsy water is used for washing the air-cleaner units and other hand washables, or most of it is scooped into pails for other cleaning — washing the car, household surfaces, or garden tools. The remaining sudsy water is used for washing out the cleaning rags. The clear water in the other tub is kept for anything that needs rinsing or for watering inside plants. I gather water from either tub by the pail for the garden. Outside, the soapy water has the added benefit of softening my clay soil. Save water and lift weights. Can't be bothered? It takes less time than going to the gym. And you're being paid for it in money saved.

Like many people in my city, I don't like the taste of our water. But I can't understand why people buy bottled water considering the time, effort, and cost involved. You have to make repeated trips to the store and back. I wouldn't want to keep lugging those heavy cases of bottles or huge water cooler refills to my car, out of the trunk, and into the house. Then where do I store them? Heave them down to the basement? There's an easier and cheaper alternative. I had an under-the-sink filtration system installed that supplies lead-free, clean, and tasty water the instant I want it. The unit cost just over $100, and yearly replacement filters are about

$40. One water filter manufacturer states that its system equals 378 bottles of store-bought water. And be aware that all bottled water isn't necessarily from a spring. At least one major company simply takes tap water, filters it, packages it, and charges you more than three times the cost of using your own water, purifier, and bottles. I keep a pitcher of water in the fridge, and, if I want to take water with me on an outing, just before I leave I fill a sterilized recycled bottle and go. Recycle, and own, don't rent.

"Phone" is one expense that you can reduce. For residential lines, I find that the basic service meets my needs, so that's all I pay for. I own my phones as opposed to renting them. I don't suggest buying used phones or even refurbished ones, because I've been disappointed with them.

As for the multiple add-on services phone companies provide, I see them as an exceptionally detrimental, habit-forming expense with little enhancement to lifestyle in relation to cost. To me, they're like bank service charges. Just a way of taking people in by using psychological ploys such as "It's *only* a little more per month" as well as "you *deserve* these services because you and your time are sooooo important." Just like when you've been specially selected (along with everyone else in the phone book) to become an elite gold-credit-card-carrying member, as long as you pay the high yearly fee. The phone company also knows that, if you get used to having a product or service, you'll keep paying for it. That's why daily newspaper publishers offer free or discount trial periods, just long enough for the habit to form. Even if you don't really want to continue with the subscription, you'll delay cancelling it because you're just too busy and can't be bothered. Sound familiar?

Here's another ploy: the scare tactic. When it comes to telephones, if one stops working, I'll buy another one. But the phone company tries to scare me into buying insurance, for *only* six dollars a month, to protect against "something unexpected" happening to my phones and wiring. But the small print on the offer states that I have to pay a minimum of a year's worth of this "insurance" at about $75 or a cancellation fee of $50 plus the monthly fees if I want to stop coverage within 12 months. So I have to pay a minimum of $56 in case "something" happens to a phone. That's assuming I even worry about my phones (do you?). *If* I need to buy another phone, I'd pay less than that. Fixing a wiring problem would be more expensive, but not if it is only a faulty phone jack. Dollar stores sell them, and Bell Canada used to teach high school students to install them. I can do it. And as for other wiring problems, how likely are they? I haven't had any problems in 22 years of having my own phone line. Does Bell advertise the numbers showing the likelihood of something happening? No. Just like insurance companies don't advertise the probability statistics along with the products they sell. Do you recognize the "What if?" fear here? Do you also see how expensive this insurance of "*only* 33 cents a day" really is? And it's only 33 cents if you keep paying for it for more than a year. It's actually $1.80 a day if you cancel it after a month. If you keep the service for three years, you'll have paid about $250 including taxes. Pretty expensive peace of mind for a phone. If you pay yourself that amount, you'll have about $260 (with ING daily interest savings), which is even better insurance. You'll have more money, and you could buy a very good phone, *if* you even need to.

Let's look at another telephone service package for about $20 per month after taxes. I can't believe anyone would pay for it. One part offers a caller display so that I can run to the phone and decide if I want to answer it. Why should I rush to a display if I want to screen calls when I can hear the person after my answering machine kicks in and at that point decide if I want to get up and take the call. People are so used to machines I think that, if they don't leave a message, the call can't be too important. And either you want to answer the phone or you don't. If you answer a call but don't want to speak to someone in particular, surely you can muster the social skills to cut it short, using only a few seconds more than it takes to go over and read a display. You're already there. The other part of the package offers message taking without the phone ringing. If I want that service, I simply unplug one phone and turn off the ringer on my answering machine. Why would I pay for that?

If you have teenagers and think you need extra phone services for them, when did they start deciding what they need? Did your parents give you everything you wanted simply because you badgered them for it? My parents, not my brother and I, decided how the phone was to be used because they were paying for it. If I was on the phone with a friend and they needed to use it, I ended my call. They could have afforded another phone line, but it wasn't necessary. Don't fool yourself thinking your parents couldn't afford it but *you* can because you earn so much more money than they ever did.

Take another look at your net disposable income versus your costs of living and your total debts. Still think extra phone services for the kids are a spending priority?

Since my parents wouldn't pay for another phone line, when I was 18 I decided to pay for my own phone, and I didn't have an allowance. If you're giving your children money so that they can "learn how to handle cash," maybe paying for their own phones should be part of their cash flow experience. Then they can decide for themselves what's really important and what isn't.

I know it doesn't look like much in savings, but there's a limit to how much you have to spend, so any savings will be better spent on your goals. And it's the combination of all the savings from all expenses that will add up to a sizeable sum. Even in the above example of the phone service package, I'd rather have the $250 cash after a year than give it to the telephone company. Use of a phone is a need. Bells and whistles are wants. How much joy do they bring relative to their cost? Will you have to earn $415 before taxes to pay for them, assuming you can even add the extra working hours? Will working more be joyful? Before all these services existed, people still enjoyed life. Maybe it's because they had their $250 for something better instead of wasting it on the "*only* 68 cents per day" service providers.

For a long-distance company, I regularly call around to see which carrier is offering the best terms for my type of use. Right now, I'm with a service that offers dime-a-minute days, nickel-a-minute nights and weekends, and no monthly fees because I pay by Visa (and receive one percent back). Before using this company, though, I signed up with one that offered bonus air miles to get the $20 free groceries. Since I rarely call long distance, it doesn't make much difference on the rates, so I look for either a really cheap cost or a really good bonus and do the math. I always ask, though, about fees for switching before changing companies. For the Internet, I use the free service at the library and one of the many free e-mail providers.

If you go through my suggested buying decision process, you'll find that Basic expenses afford the fewest opportunities for doing without them or for getting the services free. There are some possibilities for recycling, though, and keeping costs low by paying only for the most basic forms. I've also given some examples proving that owning is cheaper than renting. So there are ways to spend less money on Basics — but there are greater possibilities for savings in the next expense categories.

The total amount for Basics from month to month, then, will be fairly regular. If that amount along with your mortgage or rent payment is a large proportion of your net disposable income, you may need to consider moving to a less expensive home or apartment. From the perspective of achieving your goal of early retirement through debt reduction and savings, it's always another option.

START WITH THE BASICS

- Basics cover the cost of shelter and utilities.
- Basics are the hardest expenses to cut.
- Consider making a property assessment appeal.
- Pay expenses in advance only if it's profitable.
- Own, don't rent.
- Don't buy disposables.
- If it's not in use, turn it off.
- If you can do it, don't pay a service, pay yourself.
- Limited income means limited spending — prioritize.

CHAPTER TWELVE

THE CHALLENGE:
NECESSITIES

These are required living expenses, but they are easier to reduce than Basics.

"Food" is the first category, which probably should be stated as "Groceries," because I don't include food ordered in or meals ordered outside the home. In its most simple form, food is a daily requirement, but restaurant meals are not. Likewise, any junk food purchases are recorded in the details column so that I keep track of how much I spend on this nonessential food type, which I know I really shouldn't be buying at all. But seeing the relatively large cost for so few items does stop me from buying (and eating) too much junk food.

To cut costs in this area, think of how you approach food shopping. Using my buying decision process, first think of where you can get food free. If you're really in dire straits, consider going to a Food Bank, but that's not what I mean by finding food for free.

My solution has been to grow a garden, but my parents

are ingenious at expanding that concept. Every fall, they hike across the fields of an old abandoned farm near their summer house. The farm has an overgrown orchard, but the trees still bear fruit, and my parents pick the apples and pears for fresh eating, baking, and preserving. The fruit isn't perfect, but it isn't covered with chemicals, wax, and pesticides. And it's free. A stream runs through the back of their property, and wild grape vines grow along the banks. These wild grapes make a great jelly, and they're free too.

My mom and dad always grow a garden at their home up north and a smaller one at their other house. When I was young, I hated working on a plot at The Royal Botanical Children's Garden, but I'm grateful now for the knowledge and skills I learned there. My brother grows his own wine grapes as well as a vegetable garden, and I grow berries, vegetables, and herbs in my backyard.

The produce costs only a few dollars in seeds and plants the first year, and after that it's all free. Since I don't grow hybrids, I can save some seeds at the end of one year to grow a completely new crop the next year. Cucumber and tomato seeds are rinsed off and dried outside along with bean and pea pods. The other bushes and plants are perennial producers.

Perhaps you're thinking you just can't be bothered to plant a few seeds. And as for watering or picking — can't take the time away from the gym? If you do your own landscaping and dig a garden, you won't need the gym. Too much trouble? I choose produce that's easy to grow, low maintenance, and freezes well.

If you don't have the property for a garden, you can still

grow some plants on a sunny apartment balcony, and there are books at the library on container gardening. Check out material on hydroponics as well. Alternatively, look for a garden plot by contacting local gardening clubs or community groups.

I have a sunny, hot yard with part sand, part clay soil, so I raise only the plants that grow best under those conditions, and I grow only the foods that I like. Tomatoes. Herbs. Rhubarb. Blueberries. Currants. Garlic. Onions. Peas. Green beans. And cucumbers. My parents have the opposite growing conditions in their garden, so they plant different types of produce. Then we share our harvests and enjoy a real variety of food in both households. In fact, the currant bushes belong to my father, but they need a sunny location, so he transplanted them to my yard. Now there's a bounty of currants every year. My mother makes jelly, but I freeze the berries, and throughout the winter I mix them with my frozen rhubarb and other fruit for muffins, pies, cookies, and cobblers. Dried currants are also a great addition to my herbal teas for their flavour and vitamin C content.

The herbs I grow are mostly for cooking (basil, borage, camomile, chives, feverfew, lemon balm, mint, parsley, and sage) but also double in making teas. An excellent easy-reference pocketbook on herbs is *The Herb Book*, by John Lust. I use sage for sore throats and colds, lemon balm for morning grumpiness, and camomile to combat bouts of insomnia. It's been over 15 years since I've bought any comparable commercial remedies. The herbs are free.

Cucumbers also do well in my backyard. Last summer, I planted three hills of seeds, and the plants unexpectedly took over my lawn. I was literally knee-deep in cucumbers. I used only a third of the seed packet, which equalled about 40 cents' worth, and eventually I was giving cucumbers away to anyone who'd take them. My whole family had more than enough fresh cucumbers to eat, and my mother made 25 jars of pickles and relish from the rest.

Tomatoes are easy to grow and produce so well that I decided to start only two plants last spring — one cherry tomato for salads and one flavourful tomato for the freezer. Once the tomatoes are frozen, I use them all winter for making salsa, stewed tomatoes, spaghetti sauce, chili, and in any recipe that calls for canned tomatoes. But if I grow too many, it becomes a waste of time and effort. The year before, I had four plants, and I spent a lot of time trying to give the tomatoes away after filling my fridge and freezer. So I thought cutting back to two tomato plants would be just right. But I didn't count on the ones that came up on their own in surprising places around my yard. I didn't have the heart to tear them out, so last year I had another bountiful crop of tomatoes. My kitchen was a sea of red. There were tomatoes everywhere: on top of the fridge, windowsill, table, counter, and stove. Other years, I've found onions and garlic growing among my flowers. This year, I waited to see what sprouted for free before planting any seeds.

All the plants that I have now were very easy to grow. My mother likes to say that everything grows at my place, but the truth is that some plants died, and I didn't replace them. That would have taken time and effort — and for what? More dead plants? I think it's better to work with nature than against it.

Try starting with the plants that I've found easy to grow. It couldn't be more simple: plant, water, pick, wash, and eat or freeze. I think it takes less time than driving to the store, looking over the produce, pushing the cart around, waiting in the checkout line, carrying the bags to the car, driving home, unloading the bags, and putting it all away. The biggest difference, though, is that your own garden produce can be fresher, tastier, and organic, without the expense!

I'm sure there are many other foods that are as easy to grow. I just haven't tried them due to my growing conditions or, more to the point, because I don't like them. Yellow beans come to mind. See what your neighbours grow. Chances are they'll be happy to give you some plants or seeds. Regardless, a few packets of seeds won't cost much.

Freezing my harvest ensures smaller grocery bills over the next three seasons. I've never done home canning because I think it's too much work. Let's be realistic. If I enjoyed it, maybe then, and it would be cheaper than buying the produce at the store. But I have friends and family who like canning, and I gratefully reap the rewards of their efforts anyway. But it all evens out — I give away a lot of my plants and produce to others.

So, for me, growing and storing food has to be simple. You don't have to become a farmer to save money. It doesn't have to take a lot of time or effort. If it did, I wouldn't be doing it. But with rhubarb, currants, blueberries, chives, parsley, sage, onions, garlic, and tomatoes, food storage couldn't be simpler: wash them, bag them, freeze them. That's it. No peeling, no blanching, no cooking, no mixing syrup. I recycle the smaller milk bags instead of buying "freezer bags." They're just plastic bags, after all. Surprisingly, the berries aren't mushy when they thaw. And I'm pretty pleased with myself when I see blueberries at four dollars a quart in January.

Onions and garlic are easily stored all winter in a dry, cool, dark place, preferably in a cold cellar if you have one. I use shelves in an unheated part of my basement for a pantry. Right after harvesting, onions and garlic should be left outside to dry in the shade. Last summer was the first time I tried growing a few rows of them, and after a couple of days of drying outside they seemed hard enough, so I took them inside. Big mistake. Even though I stored them in a cool, dry place in my basement, by the next morning an overpowering onion smell filled my house like a gas. As usual whenever disaster strikes, I called my father, telling him, "My house reeks from the onions. How long was I supposed to leave them outside?" He answered, "You know how they look in the store — when the outer skin is crisp. How long were they out there?" I said, "Two days." Silence, then an explosion of laughter. I had to wait and listen to him tell my mother in the background and then endure her peals of laughter. From what I could make out between their guffaws, I thought I heard the words "stink bombs," and I gathered that it would take about six weeks. Out they went. Now I know better.

Growing a garden is one way to save money, but the next step is to decide if you really need or want a particular food item. Health concerns should play a part in that decision, but usually it's a question of doing without the packaging, name brand, and processing to save money rather than not buying the basic product at all. Again, it's looking at the product for what it really is. For example, why would you buy a box with individual packets of instant oatmeal when you can buy a large (reusable) bag of the same product for a third of the cost? Convenience? Besides fewer trips to the store, it takes the same amount of time to rip open a packet and pour the oatmeal in a bowl as it does to scoop it out of a bag and pour it in a bowl. Same pouring of water. It's ready from the kettle or from the microwave in under two minutes. What's the difference except the cost and the amount of garbage produced?

I've found that most store-brand products are equivalent to brand-name products. Check the label for the manufacturer's address. If it's the same as that for a higher-priced item, then both products were likely made at the same plant. And if you try the food but don't like it, there's usually a toll-free number on the package to call the manufacturer and complain. I do that every time I'm not happy with something. Whenever I call and the customer service rep asks for my phone number, I always shrink a little when I hear "Is this Ms. Nahirny?" But they're always nice and send me more than enough in reimbursement to cover a replacement and the inconvenience I suffered.

If you must buy a higher-priced name brand product, at least buy it at a discount food store. And you can take your own bags to the supermarket and ask for a discount at the cash line — the going rate in my city is five cents per bag. It's next to nothing, but think of the environment. Don't forget that you can pay for your groceries with your set-limit credit card that offers cash back. Why pay more?

I don't like getting up early to lug the trash can out to the sidewalk, and, since most of the food I buy is in its most original form, I have very little garbage to take out and usually only need to every other week. In the winter, I haul it out once every three weeks since the cold keeps what little I have in the can from smelling. I have a composter, and I recycle store bags of all sizes along with containers, plastic wrap, and waxed paper. In the microwave, bowls and dishes act as covers, not disposable cling film. I even recycle (milk) freezer bags.

My food inventory resembles a pioneer's pantry: a huge bag of whole wheat flour, a smaller one of white flour, oatmeal, molasses, sugar, tea, pickles, salt, baking soda, vinegar. Fruit, vegetables, and bulk portions of meat and poultry are "preserved" in the freezer. I also have an extra-large bag of powdered milk for baking. These basics allow reduced spending on food. I can buy these products in economy sizes because of their long life on the shelf and in the freezer. It means fewer shopping trips, fewer impulse buys, and less food wasted.

Preparing food from scratch doesn't have to take longer than convenience foods. There are great recipes I use for quick microwave meals and mix-in-the-pan desserts. For main meals, I do a "first-Sunday-of-the-month cookfest" and freeze most of the food. This way I save time and hydro costs. I also have a bread machine, and, while it may not save money versus bought bread, it pays great dividends in healthy ingredients and flavour, not to mention the heady aroma of freshly baked bread filling the house. The only other small kitchen appliance I use regularly is a two-dollar 1950s chrome juicer that I bought at a church rummage sale. It's manual, but there's nothing like freshly squeezed juice. At grocery stores in the summer, I check for specials on citrus fruits (including the tables of reduced-price produce), bring bags of them home, squeeze, and (you guessed it) freeze most of the juice for the winter. Just add water (filtered, of course) and sweeten to taste. Easy, healthy, and cheap — but good.

More economical and efficient food purchases mean fewer trips to the store, so you'll save money on the next category of necessary expenses: "Transportation." It's unlikely you'll be able to get around for free, but there are many ways to save money in this category. Again, the question is, do you really need transportation to the extent you think you do, or do you just want it? Look at the big picture and consider it in the context of achieving your more important goals. Is there an alternative? Can you reduce your need for getting around? Not having to work makes a big reduction in the need for transportation. And do you really need the highest-priced, feature-filled, prestige-model vehicle? Is it value for your money in terms of your financial freedom?

I didn't own a car until I was 32, and there were two reasons for that decision. First, I had easy alternatives: public transit, cabs, and car rental agencies. I chose to use the bus and cabs because of my second reason: I'm a white-knuckle driver. But I'm not worried about my own driving, it's everyone else's that scares me. I finally did buy a car, though, believing I'd get over that fear in time. After researching various consumer reports on cars, I decided to buy one of the roomier small cars, a Dodge Shadow. It was during the winter, and

Chrysler was offering that model at a good price. Not surprisingly, I saw the purchase of a car only from the standpoint of adequate size, repair history, and suitability. I needed it to get around and transport fairly large loads. But it had to be reliable, so I bought it new.

Before I signed any purchase agreement, though, I checked with four dealerships for the best price. I didn't need optional features or financing. When it came to negotiating the deal, I thought it was in my best interest to have a man along, and, since my father was in sales, who could be better? At the car lots, he didn't really say much, but his presence and demeanour helped (it's hard to impress my father). I wasn't smiling much either, because I really didn't want to buy a car. But the salesmen knew I was a good customer: I was serious, and I had cash.

My father and I narrowed our search to the two dealerships that offered the lowest prices, and one Friday evening in January we paid them a visit. The two lots were just down the street from each other, and we leisurely went back and forth, bringing the price of the car down a little each time. One salesman finally told me through clenched teeth that he couldn't go any lower. So we went back to the other dealership, and I told the salesman that the lot down the street had offered a slightly better deal. I asked him what he could do for me. He left us to discuss the price with the sales manager one more time. It was getting late, but my father picked up a magazine, and I took a paperback out of my purse, and we settled back in our chairs and started reading. We were in no hurry. After a few minutes, the salesman rushed back into the office, his face flushed red. He showed me a new lower figure and waited for my answer. I took my time to consider the amount. Then I looked disappointed and asked, "Is this really the best you can do?" He stared steadily at me and said tensely, "That's it." I sat there looking around the deserted dealership, at the blackness outside, thought about it, and then asked my father, "What do you think?" He shrugged and answered, "It's up to you. It's your money." I looked back at the intense salesman. He didn't appear to be breathing. It was time to close the deal, so I said "Okay" and bought the car. My car insurance salesman knew the people at that dealership, and he later heard about the deal. He told me they hadn't made much on the sale. I probably didn't endear myself to them either. They didn't send me a calendar the next year.

A word about financing. You really need to work out the numbers. If it looks as though you'll be better off earning interest on your money and taking the dealership's low-rate financing option, be sure to consider the after-tax return on your investment. As well, you need to make calculations based not only on the rate of interest charged but also on the length of the term. You could easily end up paying more in total payments at a lower rate of interest over a longer term than you would by paying a higher rate of interest over a shorter term. Do the math.

The car served its purpose over the next seven years. It was convenient, but I still hated driving. At one point, it was stolen from my driveway on a weekday afternoon, and it was a hassle handling the police report, the car rental, the recovery of my car, and the auto body shop. I discovered that my model of car was very easy to steal. So I had to get an antitheft device.

I retired a few years after buying the car, and, since I used it very little, I began to resent paying for insurance that was relatively high even though I used the car for "pleasure only." And then, on one of my infrequent trips, my car was badly dented in a parking lot. It was a hit and run, leaving $350 in damage that I had to pay for. My desire to own a car was wearing thin. It was time to research the alternatives.

I had a few options. I could stand taking a bus if it was for short distances and if I didn't have to travel during rush hour. I could go by cab, but I've never liked cabs. I could rent a car whenever I needed one, but then I'd have to drive. My brother suggested that I get a bike, and that's how my neighbour gets around, but I couldn't see myself biking around the city. All of these alternatives worked out to be cheaper than keeping my car after I considered the number of times I've needed it since retirement. You may not require two vehicles, or even one, when you're retired. There are other options.

But I didn't find any of the above solutions particularly attractive. Then, as I was walking home one afternoon from the library, I noticed a chauffeur helping an elderly lady out of a car and then carrying her shopping bags into her house. What a great solution for me! I phoned a few limousine services and found out that, if I was a regular customer, they would charge me "corporate" rates as opposed to more expensive special occasion rates. Apparently, some businesspeople were regular clients, and I'd have the same conservative but classy service that they enjoyed. I didn't want an ostentatious limousine. And I had a choice: I could opt for either the service package of a car and a uniformed driver or just the car and pay the driver separately. I discussed the number of trips, time involved, and flexibility I could offer, and a limousine turned out to be a little more expensive than a taxi but still cheaper than keeping my car. Trips out of the city would be exorbitant, but I really needed a car only locally. I made my decision. When my insurance came up for renewal, I got rid of my car.

I realize that my solution may not work for your situation, but maybe when you're retired. . . . Regardless, the point is to check out viable alternatives to save money. You might be pleasantly surprised at what you find out.

Under "Personal" expenses, I include medical, dental, and any other necessary personal care item. Interestingly, now that I'm retired, I seem to spend much less on prescriptions and over-the-counter drugs. My only conclusion is that I must be happier and healthier. So try to live a healthier lifestyle now. It should save you some money. Otherwise, use the same buying decision process as for food. Can you get it free (herbal teas)? Can you live without it? (Do you really need to have your teeth checked twice a year? Ask your dentist.) Also, the benefits of some products are questionable at best. Perhaps you're just buying another bottle of snake oil. Can you buy it at a discount (generic, discount retailer, bulk buy)?

I'm annoyed at how many products and services are more expensive simply because they're promoted to women. Recently, I bought a "men's" antiperspirant because the main ingredient matched that in the higher-priced "women's" product. If I'm buying unscented antiperspirant, what's the difference? Yes, I felt silly picking up the he-man product, but I'd have felt sillier still if I paid twice as much for the same thing, the only difference being that the more expensive product's label targets the sex that gently glows. Besides, if the label really bothered me, I'd just peel it off and turn the antiperspirant into a no-name product. In the same way, could you recycle another item to meet your needs or buy one standard, cheap, multiuse product (e.g., cotton swabs for ears, makeup, and household paint touch-ups)?

As for prescriptions, my doctor is aware that I don't have a drug plan, so he requests the less expensive generic brand, and decides on the highest quantity, so that I pay only one dispensing fee. My constitution seems to be sensitive, so, if he advises that I can try half a pill first to see if it works, that's all I take, and that way I get two pills for the price of one. Some medications just don't come in lower doses, so then my only choice is to cut the pills in half. *Warning:* my medical complaints have been relatively insignificant, so *check with your own doctor before trying anything like this.* One time my doctor became very upset with me for stopping a medication too soon after I felt better. Don't make any changes in taking medication without the advice of your doctor first! Ask, ask, ask. And don't forget to phone around for the pharmacy with the lowest dispensing fee and preferably free delivery. I've found the fees to vary by as much as $10. For 15 minutes of checking, that equals $40 an hour tax-free!

The next category, "Household" expenses, includes everyday maintenance costs such as small repairs, cleaning and other household products, and supplies. Larger renovations or big decorating projects should be considered Unusual costs.

I used to buy many different cleaning products for my house because I saw my mother using them when I lived at home, and I just assumed I needed them too. Then I met a professional cleaning lady who told me that she uses only vinegar, rags, and hot water for most jobs. So I tried it. I've found that vinegar works just as well, if not better, than most of the commercial sprays, liquids, and powders that I used to buy. Vinegar is much cheaper — and there's no tax on it! Try mixing vinegar with hot water first, but if the mixture isn't cleaning well pour in more vinegar. Don't combine it with any other product. Vinegar not only cleans well but also eliminates odours. Forget the foam shower cleaner — have you noticed how one brand uses "*daily* shower cleaner" as a subliminal message both on the label and spoken in the commercials? If you're subtly brainwashed into believing that the product has to be used *daily*, wouldn't you have to buy it more often? Instead, after each shower, I make a few swipes across the tiles with a squeegee. Decide for yourself what you need and how often to use it — and save money.

Don't buy disposable cleaning products! Paper towels, broom sweeper sheets, as well as plastic buff and mesh scrubbers shouldn't be on your shopping list. Cleaning brushes of all sorts are under a dollar each at discount stores and last forever. Cut up free plastic mesh produce bags into squares and wrap an elastic band tightly around the centre. Instant scrubber. Your broom doesn't need a sleeve — that's what bristles are for. Use rags for dusting and cleaning and free paper instead of paper towels. My free paper comes from flyers, old phone book pages, tissue gift wrap, and newspapers. I keep torn squares of it near the sinks. I use the recycled paper to wipe off greasy pans and messy plates before washing them, so I don't have to buy drain cleaner or put the dishes through the wash cycle twice. I reuse pieces of old towels for spills instead of buying package after package of paper towels.

Try buying in bulk. I have ceiling-height shelves in the basement beside my "pantry" for bulk dry goods. Whenever there's an exceptional sale on, I pick up the huge family size or large packs of toothpaste, soap, detergent, vinegar, and of course toilet paper. Walking up to the cash register and out of the store with cargo-sized buys of toilet paper is a tad embarrassing, but if you're going to save money you can't care what people think. If I had, I wouldn't be retired.

When buying in bulk, make sure the product has a long shelf life, really is less expensive, and is what you'd regularly buy anyway. Also watch for products sold in "premeasured" sizes. I've found that the recommended amount has always been more than I needed. Do you think a manufacturer might want you to use more and buy more that way? I made this discovery when I had a coupon for a trial can of dishwasher detergent "tabs." I have a small dishwasher, so I cut the tablets in half first, but half was still too much. I could taste the cleaning agent residue on the glasses even after they'd been through the proper rinse cycle. So, for my use, one-third of a tablet is just right. One-third the price, one-third the taxes. Think about it the next time you use any manufacturer's product premeasured for your *convenience*. Convenient? It's more expensive.

Some household expenses, though, can't easily be avoided

or reduced. My present house stood vacant for quite a while as it was being renovated. During that time, I couldn't have known about the centipedes multiplying prolifically in my future home. But when I moved in, they were there to greet me. Every night, families of them made the pilgrimage up from the basement to the top floor just as I was about to turn out the lights. They'd scurry up the walls and trundle across the floor, and could they *move!* I had to aim at a point ahead of where I thought they were going to make sure that my fist met their bodies. There was never time to get a tissue — it was pound them or lose them. If I missed, they'd run behind the baseboard, and I would lie awake all night wondering when they were going to come out and crawl across my covers. One morning I awoke to find the flattened remains of a spider stuck to my sheet, so I knew it was only a matter of time before a centipede ended up in bed with me. The smaller ones weren't so bad, because I could effectively rub them out with my thumb, but I lost sleep over knowing that the really big ones were hiding, waiting for nightfall to pay me a visit. I tried spraying the house with a can of pesticide, but I had an infestation. One night I counted 13 of them travelling together up the basement stairs. It was serious. To keep my sanity, I called in a professional exterminator, who came over and got rid of the bugs. While he wasn't cheap, he did guarantee his work. That was enough value for my money.

Some household expenses are worth every penny, but think about the alternatives, determine exactly what you need, and try doing the job yourself first. A local building supply store may offer free classes on general home repairs and improvements. Check for free videos and how-to books at your local library. Ask people you know for help. Keep in mind, though, that the best savings of all may be in hiring a pro. Unskilled jobs around the house are easy ways to cut expenses, but if a job requires specialized skills you're probably better off to call a professional.

The last necessity is "Insurance." It is possible to cut costs, but you must be able to assess your level of risk. Find out from insurance agents not only the perils they cover but also the statistics showing the probability of the events actually happening. I think they'll hesitate to give you that information. But without it, how can you judge if you'll be getting value for your money? A little research into life insurance, property insurance, and auto insurance will pay off. A better understanding of what your policies cover can help you save money.

For instance, I decided on a less expensive standard policy to insure my home and property that generally only covers major losses. If my freezer stops working and the food spoils, my policy doesn't cover the loss. But I don't care, because the possibility of that happening is remote, and I don't intend to make small claims. While working at an insurance broker's office, I noticed that some insurers refused to renew policies where too many claims had been made. And multiple small claims seemed to raise policy rates. Since then, I've decided that I need insurance only to cover major losses, and that's all I'm willing to pay for. If you have a comprehensive homeowner's policy, read it carefully and consult with your broker or agent. Decide if you want to pay for all the types of coverage and if you'd even make a claim if a certain loss occurred.

Separate "riders" added to policies for specific personal effects can be very expensive, so make sure the items are valuable enough to you to insure them this way. Also make sure that they're not already covered under your general policy. However, it's just as important to be certain that you're not underinsured. Call your insurance company about having an evaluation so that in the event of a loss your replacement costs for property and rebuilding are well protected.

I'm currently with a direct insurer that bypasses the third-party insurance broker. Every year I call at least three insurance providers, and so far the direct companies have offered the most insurance for the least money. But I'm comfortable eliminating the middleman only because of my experience from working at an insurance office and because I've been through the claims process. I wouldn't suggest that you go the direct route unless you really understand insurance products, are familiar with the claims process, and can make well-informed decisions concerning your insurance needs. Otherwise, find an agent at a broker's office. Then you'll have an advisor who can compare a few different insurers' rates on your behalf. Alternatively, you could call various insurance companies on your own to compare rates and, when you find the best value, look for a broker who deals with that company. Any agent there will be able to give you a valuable opinion on the company's insurance products.

To reduce my risk of loss, and in turn lower insurance costs, I have a home alarm system and working smoke detectors in the basement and on both floors. I also keep the house well maintained. My deductible is relatively high to further decrease the insurance rate. But one of the best ways to save money is to make it difficult for your property to be stolen. When my house was robbed, the police officer who handled the report warned me that thieves often come back. The thieves who broke into my house must have been sorely disappointed with the takings, because they didn't try again. Still, I was worried at the time, and I asked the officer for advice. She suggested that, besides a home alarm, I should get a dog or at least buy the biggest dog dish I could find and keep it on the back porch. But it had to look "for real." So I bought a huge plastic dog bowl, and the closest prop I could find for food was a handful of brown landscaping stones. They're cut in puffy squares and look remarkably like kibble, but they don't attract ants or turn mushy in the rain. I even considered painting a former boyfriend's name on the bowl, and it was very fitting, but in the end I charitably decided against it.

All my basement windows have bars on them now, the house is outfitted with a complete alarm system, there are extra locks on windows and doors, and I feel much more secure. Anyone intent on breaking in could still do so, but it would be done to much fanfare, and the would-be thief would soon find out there isn't anything conventionally profitable to take.

As for auto insurance, when I had it I made sure I received all the discounts available to me. I also called around every year and went with a direct insurer. Right after my car was stolen, another insurance company offered a free antitheft device and matched the best rates I could find, so I switched over to that company. The next year, when it raised its rates, I phoned around and took my business to a cheaper direct insurer, getting a discount for the free antitheft device. Make sure your agent tells you which part of your policy is mandatory under the law and which charges are optional. Understand the options and decide if you want the coverages. For a few years, I took coverages off my car during the worst winter-driving months, knowing that I wouldn't be driving anyway. The reimbursed money covered cab fare and a few other purchases for those months.

You need to make a thorough review of your life and disability insurance policies. First take a look at the coverages you have with your employer. Discuss them with your insurance agent, keeping in mind the coverages you personally want. The agent's advice is to be seriously considered, not blindly taken. Although I needed and received disability insurance in the past, it doesn't apply to my circumstances now, but I am looking into supplementary health insurance. I've never bought life insurance since there's no one who needs to be provided for in the event of my death. I think that I have enough assets to cover my funeral, and as far as I'm concerned I don't really care about the particulars. I'll be dead. Obviously, planning for death is a very personal choice, and, if you have dependants, it's a much more serious one. Educate yourself with books and consult an advisor. It is important.

Saving money on insurance products is more difficult than saving money on consumer products, simply because the area of insurance coverage is far more complex. Take comfort, though, that expenses in the next category, Variables, are the easiest of all to reduce.

NECESSARY SAVINGS

- Grow produce at home or in a community garden.
- Buy food in its most basic forms.
- See transportation only as a way of getting around.
- Know your options and calculate the costs before buying.
- Let product use, not advertising, guide purchasing.
- It can be false economy not to hire a professional.
- Research your insurance needs thoroughly.

CHAPTER THIRTEEN

THE CHALLENGE:

VARIABLES

Once you've determined the expenses you require for living (i.e., needed for basic survival), all the remaining ways that you spend your money are recorded under Variables. Your expense headings may be different from mine, but they will still be the costs that offer the widest range of potential savings, simply because spending patterns in these areas reflect wants, not needs. On my Monthly Expenses chart, I label these costs as Furnishings, Gifts, Clothing, Recreation, and Hobbies.

I define "Furnishings" as any purchase that improves my home environment aesthetically and can be taken with me when I move. These buys become my personal effects, are ongoing, and are purely for pleasure. Large essential pieces of furniture are recorded under Unusual expenses because they're durable goods and won't be regular monthly costs. Likewise, paint and wallpaper are "Household" expenses because they remain with the house, and the cost won't be repeated often. Furnishings are all the small ways that I enhance my decor.

If you've followed my suggestion to reduce the clutter in your home, you should be surrounded by the furnishings that please your senses. Fresh flowers are one of the few accessories that need to be replaced regularly, but you can save money easily by growing your own, buying potted plants, or getting cut flowers at grocery stores rather than expensive florist shops. You'll need a good light source to grow your own flowering plants indoors, but Christmas cactus and African violets started from free cuttings are easy, and spring bulbs saved each year and replanted the next do well too. From April to November, there are always some flowers or bushes blooming in my yard that I can bring in for cut flower arrangements. During December and January, I trim branches from the various evergreens outside and bring vases full of greenery inside. By the end of January, though, I keep an eye open for inexpensive potted flowers usually found at the local farmer's market or "on special" at florists and discount grocery stores.

The first part of this book has already covered how I saved money by sewing or using my staple gun and glue gun to make soft furnishings, ranging from cushions to drapes. There were a few reupholstering projects as well. An aunt was throwing out an old ottoman because the "leatherette" had torn in a few places. I rescued it and used the good sections of some damaged drapery fabric for the recovering job. It took two hours to finish it, and I had a new piece of furniture with the added feature of extra storage. I've never considered my work to be at a professional level, but who cares? If it looks good and serves its purpose, it's just fine. No one has scrutinized my craftsmanship yet. Best of all, it saves a lot of money.

Other accessories can be found at garage sales, flea markets, local charity shops, or dollar and discount stores. I've found so many beautiful things that originally were very expensive but somehow ended up being discarded. Usually, the quality is better at a resale shop than at bargain stores, but it always depends on the item. Coloured glass accessories are fine from an inexpensive import store, but they could be cheaper still at a hardware store, thrift shop, or yard sale. Don't forget that another important benefit of buying used is the tax savings.

I have some relatives who hunt for finds on garbage collection days, but I just can't do it. Not even under the cover of darkness. I wish I could. They've managed to scrounge amazing treasures. Of course, garbage picking in some locales is against the law, so if you're going touring make sure there isn't a bylaw against it where you live. Some areas have occasional "big garbage" or "reuse it" days when everyone is supposed to take unwanted but usable goods to the curb. Find out if your community has anything like that. But whether you're trying to find something free or low cost, you should be looking only for the specific things you want. Otherwise, your home will become cluttered again, filled with "bargain" junk and garbage.

Garage sales and thrift stores are my favourite haunts. If I'm looking for a Blue Willow vase, it will probably be finer quality there than at a dollar store. If it has a small chip, a little "plaster mend" compound and a little paint are all it needs. Usually, though, the foliage will cover any faults, or I'll turn the china with its flawed side to the wall. When furnishings are imperfect and inexpensive, I'm not upset if they break: they're easily replaced.

Surplus stores are good for finding small electronics such as clock radios, telephones, and answering machines, but I'd stick to major brand names. These retailers are always bringing in a variety of stock, so look for bargain prices on home improvement supplies, kitchenware, and tools of all kinds as well.

Try to get your furnishings for as little as possible by finding them free, making them yourself, or buying them used. There may be some surprises in store for you. When I landed my first full-time job, my mother told me that I should buy something nice for myself from every paycheque just because I was working. My grandmother had told my mother the same thing. I interpreted the word "nice" as "expensive," and that meant silver pieces to me at the time. On my lunch hours, I'd shop in the fine-silver department at the Eaton's store in downtown Hamilton. One time, a set of silver teacups caught my eye. The saucers and cup holders were filigree silver, and the cups were glass. They were $20 each, a lot of money compared with my disposable income, so I could only afford to buy two. Over the next 15 years, I was sorry I hadn't bought a couple more. I didn't see them again until a charity shop opened near my home. Naturally, I went to the Amity Goodwill grand opening but hid my face when the local television station filmed the throng. Me? Shop at a thrift store? I didn't want to advertise the fact, so I made my way to the back of the store, where the glass and china were on display. Among the bits and pieces were two of those silver-and-glass teacups in perfect condition. They were meant for me — and they were $1.99 each!

Last year, I started looking for a wicker bed tray. Sears priced them at about $50 in its catalogue. I wasn't about to pay that much. I searched garage sales and local resale shops, but to no avail. Then I went shopping with a friend to a more distant Amity. She managed to find an assortment of golf bags and chose a lovely leather one. I hadn't come across anything I wanted, but a crowd was gathering at a cordoned-off area. Luckily, I'm tall, and I was able to see that the others were eyeing a fresh truckload of donations being unloaded behind the rope. Among the junk was a white wicker bed tray! I knew that tray was mine. I stood poised at the front of the line, tensely waiting, engulfed by fierce determination. No one else had a chance. When the rope was released, I shot over to the tray, snatched it, and hugged it all the way to the cash register. It cost 59 cents.

So try the cheaper alternatives. You'll spend the same amount of time shopping at an expensive store and may not even find what you want. Start at the bottom. You won't know what's out there until you look.

Over the past few years, gift buying has become much easier in my family. While I consider total Christmas spending to be an Unusual expense since it happens only once a year, I'll cover money-saving techniques for holiday presents here. Generally, now that everyone in my immediate family is over 40, we find that we don't really need anything. So we exchange small luxury gifts. My father has always been hard to buy for, and one year he stated in his practical manner, "If I can't eat it or drink it, don't waste your money." Gourmet foods and good wines have taken on greater importance for gift giving now. We select specialty foods that we wouldn't normally buy for ourselves, and, if they're not to our taste, there aren't any hurt feelings when they get tossed out. And we can spend more on the gifts because many food items are tax-free. It's also fun to share and enjoy all this luxury fare together.

I know some people who recycle gifts, but I'd rather not, and I'll tell you why: I've had the experience where my gift was given to someone else right in front of me. It was a shower present of expensive crystal, carefully chosen for the woman's taste and decor. She was well aware that I was going to be a guest at the next woman's shower, and in fact many of the same people were there when she gave away my present. Later, a few of the guests said to me, "Wasn't that the same crystal you gave her?" Saving money is fine, but let's be kind about it.

There are so many places to find gifts for little money. At some supermarkets with adjacent floral shops, you can choose gourmet foods from the grocery aisles and then have the florist make up a gift basket for you. Some will even deliver the basket for a small charge. Better still to buy the food at a discount grocer, find a basket at a garage sale or charity shop (for under a dollar), and save even more on materials and taxes. If you don't have any recycled cellophane or tissue paper, buy it at a dollar store, make the gift yourself, and save the charge for labour. Or you could take your own base to a florist to have a special flower arrangement created. The base could have sentimental value to the recipient or be a collectible you've found at a garage sale or resale shop.

I found a perfect birthday gift for my brother one year at an outdoor flea market. When we were growing up, Mom did a lot of baking, and she had an unusual cookie jar that was always filled with her homemade treats. Unfortunately, it was broken beyond repair when we were teenagers, but our fond childhood memories of it stayed with us when we were adults. On that outing to the flea market, I spied Mom's cookie jar at the end of a table. It was in excellent condition, with the same raised pattern of multicoloured cookies all over the jar and one in the centre of the lid for a handle. It wasn't terribly expensive, but the price didn't matter — it made me smile, and I had to have it. I knew my brother would be surprised and like the sentiment, but I had trouble deciding if it was for his birthday or if it was for me. In the end, I wanted to see the look on my brother's face, and I knew he'd really like it, so I gave it to him. Besides, if I ever want a reminder of those cookie jar memories, I know where it is.

"Clothing" as the next expense is really a need, but if you look at most people's spending patterns it reflects a want. Generally, clothes are bought according to style, colour, fabric, label, feel, trend, and desired emotional response, not solely based on the need to be covered up. But that's all right, because once you recognize exactly what you want from your clothes you can find them free or inexpensive and still have your wants met. Clothing accessories and cosmetics are included in this category since they are worn for the same purposes and can cost less.

Before I buy any new clothes, I check through my wardrobe and decide what I need (i.e., want) and take a look at the new fashion magazines (free from the library) to pick out the styles I like. Then I start from the bottom. Is there anything

I want that I can get free? This is where my friends and family come in. We have our own informal clothing exchange. It's normal for us to visit each other carrying bags of stuff we don't want anymore, but it's all still good! Fortunately, my best friend, my sister-in-law, and I are about the same size, so we trade clothing regularly. Size doesn't matter for scarves, purses, and jewellery, though. I've even rescued a shirt of my brother's that was in the garbage but looked perfectly good to me. I asked my brother if he was throwing it out by mistake, and he told me to look at the elbow. Sure enough, it had a hole, but I've found men's shirts to be much better quality and far more comfortable than women's shirts, so I still wanted it. I just rolled up the sleeves (why waste time sewing?), and it's been perfect to wear when I'm gardening or sculpting with clay. I have a few shirts of my father's too that have become art smocks and home improvement coveralls.

Most other freebies need alterations of some kind, but they're always minor, and I do them myself because, if I ruin the article, it doesn't matter. Usually, the extent of the fixing is filling in scratched leather with coloured markers, shoe polish, or dye; hemming, changing buttons, or taking in a few seams; or dying fabric a new colour or redying it the same colour to make the garment look new. Dye costs about a dollar, as do marking pens, shoe polish, and thread at bargain stores.

As for cleaning, I wash many "dry-clean only" clothes if I think the fabric will withstand it. Only twice has it not worked out. The colours on one silk blouse ran together, and a rayon skirt shrunk. Try rug shampoo on fabric stains — I've had some success with it. But every year, I hand-wash one of my wool jackets and hang it outside to dry because my results have been better than the dry-cleaners'. Each time, it's come back from the cleaner pilled and greyish instead of smooth and off-white, so I've been washing it myself. Drying the coat in the sun makes it the whitest it's ever been, and I iron it on the wool setting, spraying it with water first and using a press cloth (old tea towel) on top. This method seems to thicken rather than flatten the pile, and there's no orange peel pilling. So much for dry-cleaning.

If free isn't an option, think about repairs. Take shoes, boots, purses, and briefcases to your local shoe repair for an estimate. You can buy polishes, protector sprays, and dyes there, but they're probably cheaper at a discount store. Heels on shoes and boots can sometimes be changed to the latest style, making it cheaper than buying new. When I couldn't find a pair of shoes in the colour I wanted, I bought a white pair and sprayed them with shoe dye. Dark-coloured markers work wonders for small touch-ups on belts, shoe straps, and purse handles. Try finishing with an inexpensive shoe polish, floor wax, or furniture spray. They all give that "looks new" coating, and it resists stains and water spots. Be careful, though, if you get some furniture spray on the floor — it can be dangerously slippery. Whichever product you choose, let cost be your guide.

One alternative to buying clothes new is to sew them, but it's time consuming, and you need skill, a sewing machine with good attachments, and the materials (which can be expensive). My mother is a true seamstress, but my talents and patience don't match hers, so I don't make clothes from scratch. I'd much rather buy a quality garment that needs a little fixing or tailoring. And my method of tailoring is very simple. I put the clothes on inside out, mark the adjustments with pins along the seams, and carefully take the clothes off. Then I draw along the pin markings with a shard of soap (you can also use chalk or light pencil), reinsert the pins perpendicular to the line, and sew. I try each piece on again, and if it looks okay I finish by trimming away the extra fabric with pinking shears. Obviously, this isn't the professional way to tailor, but it's fast and easy and works just fine. The clothes look well fitted from the outside, and who's going to see them inside out? If I only paid five dollars for an outfit, I'm going to worry about how it looks on the inside? Again, nobody has scrutinized my workmanship yet. Get a book from the library on rudimentary sewing skills or easy tailoring just to learn the basics. Then do it yourself, look good, and save your money.

About a third of my wardrobe has come from either people I know or charity outlets. I'm often surprised by the number of quality designer labels and European-made fashions that end up in these stores. Sometimes I don't find anything I want, but when I do it's something I'd never have paid the original retail price for. And the more time you spend shopping "at the bottom," the more likely you are to find a steal, and the less likely you are to spend time and money at higher-priced stores. There's only so much time to shop. Give cheaper a chance.

When I was working full time and out of town one day, I had some time to spare, but instead of sitting in a café with an overpriced coffee I went for a walk along the main street. I passed a specialty stationery shop, a fancy perfumery, a gourmet chocolatier, and an upscale leather goods shop. Then

I came to an unobtrusive storefront, and I almost passed right by but noticed the charity's name on the door. A thrift shop! In I went. It was about the size of two walk-in closets, and there wasn't much inventory. But it was easy to check the articles for sale against the list I always carried of expensive things I wanted to buy cheaply. One of the items on my list was a soft-sided briefcase. The shop had one that was well made, of quality leather, and exactly the size I wanted. The price was right at three dollars, but the colour was wrong. It was burgundy, and I wanted black. So I bought it and that night sprayed it with a can of leftover black shoe dye. It turned out beautifully. Five years later, I had the handle replaced, then used the briefcase for work for another couple of years. Lately, it's been handy to carry around my laptop. And I was pleased to see the same style of case at a department store recently for $285. It pays to start at the bottom.

Besides shopping for clothing at resale shops, women should consider the alternative of disregarding labels and buying the basic article wherever it's the best buy. It could be in the men's department. When I lived in Toronto, my route to and from work led past some little shops in an older part of the city. On the sidewalk in front of one store was a sale rack of turtleneck sweaters, and I didn't realize they were men's until I looked in the shop window. The sweaters were $4.99, without labels but made of good-quality fabric. I picked one that looked the right size for me and debated my dilemma. I wasn't going to put it on in a *men's* change room! I finally decided to take a chance, and I bought it without trying it on. Twenty years later, it still looks great. I don't know what it's made of, but it's washable and looks like new. So, ladies, work up your nerve and check out the young men's and men's departments for socks, casual or dress shirts, jackets, jeans, and sweaters. You'll probably find good quality and a lower price. Remember to look at the item for what it basically is or does, not whom the manufacturers and marketers have decided it's for.

Finally, if you must buy clothes at a regular retailer, go where you can get something extra — bonus points, pant/skirt hangers, a sale price, or an additional discount. Last summer, I was shopping at a major department store and was about to buy a linen skirt at 50% off. I noticed a slightly pulled thread that I could easily fix, and I wrongly assumed that was why the skirt was on sale. Even so, when I went to the till, I pointed out the flaw, and the clerk gave me another 10% discount. Ask, ask, ask.

As for cosmetics and other personal care products, I've already covered how important it is to look at them for what they really are. I've used shampoo as an example. It cleans hair. Yet I've seen prices that range from $1 to $12. I can understand buying other styling products for a price, but a cleaning agent? It does its job and is washed down the drain. Don't wash your money away too.

I've been colouring my hair since I was a teenager, starting with henna and then moving on to commercial dyes in my 20s. It's a complete waste of money, but for the price I think it's fun. The only time I paid a salon to change my hair colour was when I became a blonde. It turned out to be not only more expensive but also more damaging to my hair than when I continued to keep it blonde myself. The stylist lightened the colour too much, and my hair felt like thatch. After that experience, I called the L'Oreal consumer hotline for advice on home hair colouring. The rep was very helpful, so I tried their blonding product, and it produced a much better result. I went back to the salon for a haircut, and the stylist was surprised at the excellent colouring I'd done on my own. My hair was softer and a more natural colour. But if you're going to colour your hair yourself, always heed the instructions, and do a couple of tests first. Do an allergy patch test, and try colouring a lock of your hair cut from an inconspicuous place. Then you'll know the results beforehand, which can save you from making a terrible mistake with the rest of your hair.

Consider cosmetics and other personal products in the same light. Many times, cheaper is better. And, if you don't like a product, complain to a customer service rep using the manufacturer's toll-free number or take it back to the store. Most cosmetics companies are fair about exchanges and returns. But before you buy anything, remember your new consumer behaviour. Do you need it or just want it? Can you do without it considering your more important goal of financial freedom? Can you get it free (promotions, trial samples — ask!)? What does the product really do in its most basic form? Can you do it yourself? Can you use an alternative? Where can you buy it for the lowest price (beauty supply store, catalogue, on sale, discount store)? Then, and only then, should you make a buying decision.

The next expense category is "Recreation," which includes spending on all forms of entertainment and outdoor activities. I include vacations in Unusual because they are fairly large singular expenses and only occur periodically. Monthly extracurricular costs, then, are recorded under "Recreation." For most people, this will be a big percentage of current spending. It can also be the easiest to reduce without hurting your quality of life.

Most of my sources of entertainment are free or cost next to nothing. The public library is an amazing warehouse of amusements. From home, I can reserve newly released fiction books, movies, how-to videos, CDs, and books on tape. I can also place holds on materials currently on the shelves for quick pick up at the branch of my choice. Why would you rent or buy something when you can get it free? The only exception I make is how-to magazines and books, which I buy because I know I'll want to refer to them in the future. Add up how much you've spent over the past three months on entertainment materials: all the CDs, magazines, pocketbooks, newspapers, TV guides, videos, and hardcover books you've bought. Then you'll realize just how much you've been spending. Get them free instead.

I have three televisions in my house, but two of them are the kind that doesn't have a remote. I don't enjoy cooking, so the small one in the kitchen makes meal preparation more fun. When it's turned on, it's within easy reach, so I don't need a remote. As a matter of fact, the TV was free. My father saw it on the roadside out for garbage, and, being a pro at repairing TVs, he couldn't just leave it there. It was free! He picked it up, fixed it, and gave it to me. He's done that a few times. That's how I came to own the third one for my bedroom. Yes, I actually have to get up to turn it on and off, but I suppose

I have the energy because I'm not wasting it on a job.

So-called obsolete entertainment units get that label because without it manufacturers wouldn't be able to turn over their inventories as quickly. Most of my components are from the wood grain era, but they don't get stolen, and they do serve their purpose. If they produce a great picture and excellent sound and have all the features I want, does it matter that they aren't black? If I wanted a more contemporary look, I could paint the cabinets, but I think sound and video units are ugly anyway, so they're all hidden throughout my house, which ensures that I don't see those blights on my interior landscape. New doesn't always mean better. Think about what you want from the product and then judge its value in relation to its price. Can you get it free? Is it a "gotta have it" brainwashed buy, or would you rather have freedom? Is there an alternative? Could you make it yourself? Get a book or video from the library (my brother and father have made many of their own components). Finally, where can you buy the product for less?

Take a careful look at all your recent home entertainment purchases and see if you made them automatically, without considering value for money or the free alternative. Maybe you need to make some changes in your buying behaviour.

Then look at your entertainment expenses outside the home. They include restaurant and fast-food meals, admission to sports games and other entertainment venues, and memberships at organizations, recreation centres, and health clubs.

If you're serious about finding extra cash to pay down your debts and build up your assets, you'll cut costs here, because this is where the larger regular outlays occur. Look at your spending. What was once a treat you probably now consider routine. Remember need versus want? These expenses are all wants. Remember limited disposable income? There's a restriction on the amount of cash available for you to spread among past debts, basic costs of living, necessities, planned or unexpected major outlays, and all your unlimited wants. You must make choices and trade-offs. If you're ever going to use your new money-handling behaviour, do it here! If you complain about having no time, why do you need to see the new releases at the theatres right now? They'll be around when you actually have time to enjoy them — and they'll be free at the library. Do you really have to attend sports games so often? Couldn't you cut one out and throw a ball around with your kids instead? Don't you think it would be more fun than depositing them with their minor sports league, swim team, summer camp, play school babysitters? I'm grateful that my mother and father were parents and not just chauffeurs and human cash machines. They taught me and my brother life skills. Some things we learned together. Some things we all weren't very good at, but we enjoyed laughing at our attempts. We had fun as a family. You can't pay someone for that. We did so many things, and they didn't cost much money. When was the last time you flew a kite, went on a nature hike or a picnic, took in the local sights, played cards, made some crafts or artwork with your children, built a birdhouse, or just talked and dreamed? You can't buy quality time with your loved ones — you make it. Do it yourself, do it together, and save money while you're at it. Your Balance Sheet will improve, your kids will learn something new, and you'll all profit from the memories.

You're probably wondering where you'll find the time to enjoy inexpensive activities. Cut out the gym. I know I won't gain much popularity with this viewpoint, but I can't believe people would rather spend "good money" to get in shape when free opportunities abound. It makes me think of a friend who wouldn't consider raking his leaves, cutting his grass, or shovelling his snow himself. He pays services to do these tasks for him, and then he pays a gym to let him work out. Work out at what? Pedalling mindlessly to nowhere? Running on the spot like so many caged mice? Climbing someone else's stairs and senselessly throwing away precious freedom dollars to do it? Quite an accomplishment. Perhaps it's buying social interaction, but why pay for it? Another friend of mine recently bought a house that needed some work. She had a health club membership but didn't need or want it after she found that it was more fun doing renovations and landscaping with her friends and going for healthy long walks in the fresh air with her neighbour. She's happier, healthier, and wealthier. She had fun while staying fit for free and saving money on home improvements. She had better results by choosing her own alternatives. If you want savings, realize that cutting out health clubs removes a sizeable expense. It's not just the membership cost either. There are new clothes, equipment, and a gym bag, travel and time costs, parking, extra personal care items for the locker, snack bar rejuvenators, and take-out food, because naturally there won't be time to make a meal at home afterward. Think of the time cost involved. Think of the cost of failing to use something you've paid for. And think of the alternatives. Like my friend, I work on the house and in the garden, and I walk everywhere. I've also finished an area in the basement with enough floor space for a dance studio, including a barre for ballet practice. If you must have the gym experience, consider buying, not renting, the equipment or getting a cheaper membership at your local YMCA/YWCA.

My final Variable expense is "Hobbies," because I have a variety of pursuits where the costs should be tracked. This expense covers any interests you may have that you regularly spend money on.

I bought my first computer in the early 1990s, and many people have one in their homes today. I think it's fun as well as useful to have one, and I rank it high on my list of priority luxuries. But I also think that computers detract from home decor. Frankly, they remind me too much of employment and work stations, so I have a laptop instead. It's small, portable, and easily hidden. It's also used. Big surprise?

If you're going to buy a used computer, consider one that is only about a year old, has a reputable brand name, and comes with a store guarantee. You could pay less than half the price of a new machine, but make sure it has the capacity and features you need. If you need advanced applications, such as the latest high-performance games with 3-D graphics, or you are planning to design your own web site and incorporate a video, you'll need a fast new computer. Generally, if your existing one isn't that old, increasing memory is one of the cheaper upgrades, whereas improving motherboards and processors isn't economical.

I had expert family help, so I wasn't concerned about doing

research on my own. I also knew exactly what my needs would be, and an older notebook was perfect for my intended use. On that occasion, though, my mother won the prize for practicality. My original computer was a fireproof industrial model, a big grey beast, that I bought wholesale for a song. Eight years later, it developed a problem that wasn't worth fixing, but I still wanted a computer to write this book. So my father and brother gravely engaged in a lengthy discussion about what I should buy, while I sat there hearing the clinking of cash register keys in my head. Have you ever noticed how easy it is for other people to spend your money? A few times I said, "But I only need it for word processing and home finance. . . ." My mother was the only one listening to me, and finally she said to my father, "Why don't you just give Dianne your old one and buy the new one you've been wanting?" Mother, the voice of reason. So simple. So cheap for me. Although I'll have to upgrade it soon, the laptop has served its purpose well. And since I've been able to delay a purchase for two years, I've had that time to earn a return to pay for the upgrade!

If you want to take up a new hobby, you may be able to sit in on a class before you decide to enrol in a course. Also, visit your local library for books and videos on the subject. Go to area recreation centres as well as public schools, colleges, and universities to see if they offer general-interest classes. When I wanted to learn about computers, I took a course for one semester at a nearby high school for free. Check your phone book for associations and clubs that might offer savings in your areas of interest.

Photography as a hobby can be very expensive, so I started

in a small way. I used the camera I had, borrowed a beginner's book on photography from the library, and found a gas station that offered free film with a fill-up. I didn't have a car at the time, so I asked my man of the moment to become a regular customer there. I built up a nice stash of film thanks to him, but all too soon the promotion came to an end. I found out it was over the day we went in for gas and he returned to the car empty handed.

But I don't give up that easily. Thinking that there must have been leftover film, and that maybe I could get it at a discount, I suggested the idea to my boyfriend. He rolled his eyes, sighed, but then got out of the car and walked back to the cash desk to find out for me. The attendant told him that the film had been thrown out. Hmmmm. I looked over at the dumpster behind the gas station. . . .

Very early the next morning, we drove up to the deserted gas station and parked around the back. While I scrunched down in the front seat, my boyfriend got out and heaved himself over the side of the dumpster. It seemed to take him forever, but he finally came back to the car, his jacket stuffed with film. I didn't pause to think if what we were doing was against some bylaw, but we were young and foolish, and luckily we weren't caught. I wouldn't try such a stunt now that I'm older and wiser. Mind you, I didn't do anything wrong: I wasn't the one dangling out of the dumpster; I was just the one hunched under the dashboard.

Contrary to these examples, I'm really not the Queen of Cheap. Most of the time, I don't live this way. But all these frugalities have a purpose: to provide money for my priority spending. Each time I choose to eliminate an expense or trim it to the bone, it's one that doesn't deliver any pleasure or at least not enough compared with something better that I'd rather have. Disposable products, cleaning equipment, new entertainment units, movie theatres, celebrity names, and specialty coffees are a few of the expenditures that don't bring me joy. So I'm not going to allow those kinds of costs to deplete the money I have to spend on the things that do make me happy.

On the next level, there are many things I could spend money on that I want, but I don't want them as much as priority luxuries. The Concorde. Steak and lobster. Antiques. A chauffeur. Silver. And, of course, the best luxury of all, early retirement. Your spending priorities may be different from mine, but financial freedom is a fairly universal desire. The point I'm trying to make is cut out the unimportant spending on your low-value wants so that you have more money for important spending on your high-value wants. If you want financial independence, your priorities are debt elimination and wealth accumulation. The most infallible way is by reducing your cost of living or living below your means. Trimming costs will also ensure that you'll have money for unforeseen, large, and irregular expenditures, which make up the final expense category, Unusual.

TAKE ADVANTAGE OF VARIABLES

- Variables offer the best potential for savings.
- Cut all costs that don't deliver value.
- Keep goals and priorities always in mind.
- Determine what you really want from a purchase.
- Follow the buying decision process.
- Start at the bottom when you must buy.

THE CHALLENGE:

UNUSUAL

Unusual expenses don't happen often, tend to be large out-lays, or are completely unexpected. They can be any type of cost from any category. And because they do happen, they're an excellent reason for saving cash from other expenditures.

For this category, I suggest using the same routine you now apply to other purchasing decisions. What is it you really need? What is the minimum you need? Can you get some or all of it free?

I'll use the example of television service here. The reception at my house was next to nothing, so I had the options of cable TV, tower antenna, and satellite dish. With cable, I had to pay an $85 installation charge, accept a set package of channels, and, if I rented the most basic service, pay $20 per month. The first year alone would have cost $325. I didn't want the channel package, and I didn't want to rent TV service. I could buy a satellite dish, but I still had to rent the monthly service, and I didn't need so many specialty channels. I would also have had to buy a small antenna just to get my local television station. The tower antenna, though, would supply 12 different stations clearly, including local stations, and an additional five channels depending on the weather. There was nothing to rent, just a onetime cost of $500 for parts and installation. After the second year, it would be cheaper than cable. I opted for the tower because I'd own the equipment, have free monthly service, receive only the channels I wanted, and pay far less over the long term. It's been eight years now, which means I've enjoyed my television service for about $60 a year.

Still, it was an unusual expense that needed to be covered. I pay for these types of costs by making a trade-off in some other area, most likely Variables, either for that month or over the next few months. If it's a cost I can plan for, I'll save enough money for it ahead of time. Once you are debt-free, you'll have all those previous credit payments to invest and earn a return on. That money will also be available for any unusual expenses, but first try to make trade-offs in other categories.

Ask yourself if you really need to make the expenditure. Can it be delayed? Are there any alternatives? Think of my laptop example. But there will be times that the expense is unavoidable, like when I had to call in an exterminator. I also had to have an ancient tree removed from my backyard. It was too close to the house and created problems at the foundation. As well, I was concerned that during a windstorm one of the huge branches hanging over the house would come crashing through my bathroom skylight, never mind damaging the roof. So the tree had to be removed by a professional tree service. I got three estimates, looked for the best price, and called previous customers to see if they were satisfied with the service. The job took a few days, but it turned out to be more difficult than the workers had expected, so they wouldn't finish it. My backyard was mud, logs, stump, and sawdust. The tree company owner promised a couple of times to have the crew return, but they had moved on to other jobs and didn't come back to my house. Then the owner wouldn't return my phone calls. But the consumer complaint columnist from my local newspaper did. He printed a scathing article on my plight, and right after that I came home from work to find that the job had been miraculously finished and the yard perfectly cleaned up. It's amazing what a little bad publicity can do.

I include vacations under Unusual expenses because they aren't necessary for basic survival, unless you hate your job, but then retirement is an even better choice. Surprisingly, the longer I'm retired, the less desire I have to go afar. I don't need the escape. Think about what you do on vacation. Probably whatever you feel like. Guess what? That's retirement. And since I enjoy over three months a year of summer, I have my fill of lazing in the sun and actually look forward to the change to cooler weather in the fall. I was too busy writing this spring to consider a getaway to a warmer climate, but when I was still working and paying off my mortgage I took a trip at least every other year.

One vacation to Jamaica was free. I'd travelled with a group to a horse ranch in Florida, but when we arrived the resort was in receivership. A couple of days later, half the group transferred to a coastal resort, but I was there for the heat, pool, and horseback riding, so I stayed. There wasn't much choice in meals, and the tennis court had seen better days, but there was evening entertainment, a beautiful pool, riding, and best of all very few tourists. We had the ranch to ourselves! After we all returned home, the more disgruntled vacationers filed a complaint with the tour company, and I did too because I didn't get what I'd paid for. As compensation, we were offered an all-expenses-paid trip to a Jamaican beach resort, which I naturally accepted. Always get value for your money.

Holiday costs at Christmas are another expense I include under Unusual because it's an easy way to track the costs and compare them year to year. Besides the spending on presents, which I've already covered, pay careful attention to all the holiday-related items you buy. The multitude of little expenditures can add up quickly! Consider mailing cards only to those you won't be able to extend greetings to in person. You could e-mail a message or create your own card or download one to send. One of my relatives saves postage by getting together with my mother and giving her the cards to hand deliver to the rest of us.

Gift wrap is another area where it's easy to save money. Every year, I go to a Christmas church bazaar where the women make unique gift tags, 10 cents for a dozen. Remember, items sold at these bazaars are tax-free too. Sometimes I make my own tags from the gold, silver, red, and green envelopes that I receive with Christmas cards. I tend to reuse gift bags because they last longer, and they are faster and easier to use than paper wrapping. I've found that fancy rolls of Christmas paper are more expensive, even at half price, than the coloured tissue paper I buy at discount stores for stuffing in the top of each gift bag. I also reuse bows and ribbons.

Visit your local library in November for books on holiday decorating and entertaining. Check out free holiday programs for children too. And borrow from the library's selection of Christmas videos, CDs, and fiction, free of charge. The staff will also be able to direct you to your area's community office or web site for low-cost ideas on local holiday events and entertainment.

Now that we're at the end of the regular costs of living, you have to realize that, if you really want financial independence, you have to bring your expenses down, which probably means adjusting your current consumer behaviour. If you need to eliminate debt as your first step, then you must take your emotions in hand, question your spending, and make some tough decisions. At first, it might seem like a battle, but it will be one worth fighting, because your financial freedom will depend on it.

The examples in this book are extreme, and my opinions are strong, but I've given them for a reason. My spending illustrations are meant not only to make a memorable impression but also to provide motivation. They relate to how you feel when you're faced with seemingly insurmountable problems. You think your problems are terrible until you hear of others' troubles, which are much worse, and then you're relieved because your own problems don't look so bad anymore. Likewise, after seeing the examples in this book, you shouldn't find it too difficult making your own economies. You don't have to save money in the extreme ways I and my family have. Some of the examples are a bit off-the-wall, and my intention was to make financial reading more fun. Still, if you can adapt my advice and try to save where *you* choose, you'll get into the routine of saving instead of spending. That's an important lesson. Your focus on saving money will alleviate the natural consumer tendency to overspend. Whatever ways you decide to cut expenses, your new awareness of your costs of living, combined with your attempts to reduce them, will change your focus from spending to saving. That simple act will be so beneficial. You know you need to stop unconscious spending, look at your priorities, and take control of your money. Your finances will improve, and your new consumer behaviour will become the norm. Your more economical habits will keep up the momentum, resulting in money for luxuries and further wealth building.

Now you know not only what to do but also how to do it. You're almost there. Putting it all together is covered in the next and final chapter.

PREPARE FOR THE UNUSUAL

- Delay the purchase; allow time to save for it.
- Use conscious buying behaviour.
- Get it free.
- Look at alternatives.
- Consider the long-term effects and own, don't rent.
- Get value for your money and complain if you don't.
- Avoid taxes and save on purchases.

CHAPTER FIFTEEN

FULL SPEED AHEAD

Can you see the light at the end of the tunnel? It's there. To reach it, you just need to take action.

Becoming financially independent may seem like an abstract concept, but you learn how to achieve this goal the same way you learn anything.

(1) **You see, hear, read, or reason how something is done.**
(2) **You grasp the concept.**
(3) **You learn more by doing and practising.**
(4) **You use the knowledge and take action repeatedly until it produces results.**

I've given you number 1. It should be easy to accomplish number 2. But you're on your own for the last two. Only you can decide if your efforts will be worth the final achievement. Think, though, of how many things you find easy now that seemed too difficult before you tried them. Imagine this: a 31-year-old woman on her own, with a crummy salary, who owns a ramshackle house in desperate need of major repairs. Yet five years later, without doing anything terribly spectacular, she's retired. If I could do it in my meagre circumstances, surely you'll be able to do as well, if not better, than I did. All you have to do is try.

These are the steps: assess your current financial standing, create a cash flow strategy, and work your money plan.

SEE WHERE YOU STAND

If you haven't already done it, prepare a personal Balance Sheet, Income and Expense Statement, Cash Flow Statement, and Monthly Expenses chart. You'll probably need to do the first two just once a year. Cash flow should be calculated quarterly at the very least and preferably monthly. Obviously, cost-of-living expenses are recorded throughout the month and totalled at the end. Make a note of any shortfall in income versus expenses as well as individual debts outstanding and regular debt payments. Those debts will have to go. Freedom is paid for by living within your means and by using assets, not debt, to do it.

CASH FLOW STRATEGY

Control your money. It's only a medium of exchange. It's how you decide to spend your time and effort (life) to pay for the things you need and want (goods and services). Without conscious control, you'll end up paying for previous purchases with past, current, and future dollars when you buy using credit.

Does enslavement to your employer come to mind? It's your life, but do you want to be chained to a job to pay for poor money-handling skills? You don't have to do without the purchase — just don't use credit. Use delayed gratification. It'll be gratifying when you have what you want and when you can buy more things with the interest you'd have paid to a finance company. And if you're making debt payments, how are you ever going to make savings deposits and investment purchases? Get out of debt and stop buying consumer goods on credit.

The purpose of tracking cash flow is to encourage inflows and discourage outflows of money. Look for ways to increase your income with a higher salary, tax credits and deductions, job perks, or multiple streams of income. Lower your expenditures by eliminating debts, avoiding all levels of taxation, applying my buying behaviour process, rethinking lifestyle choices, and reducing cost-of-living expenses.

Your goal is to have a healthy cash flow position, where inflows far outweigh outflows, preferably at 30–40% if you are paying a mortgage and eventually at 70% as you accelerate toward your early retirement date. Don't think for a minute that it's not possible. Look at your current income. How much is eaten away by taxes, debt and mortgage payments, and automatic or uneconomical spending? How much are you actually spending on current costs of living alone? Check your Monthly Expenses chart and recognize that Variables are easy to reduce. Add up your estimated total and express it as a percentage of net income. Does 30% still seem impossible? You need the other 70% for debt elimination, asset accumulation, and a mortgage, if you don't already own a home. Own, don't rent.

Just before my parents were married, they bought a house together. Even though they wouldn't be moving in before the wedding, my mother didn't tell her parents until the offer was accepted. I asked her why. She said, "My parents thought we should live with your father's family until we could save money for a more substantial down payment. They were afraid we would take on too much debt otherwise." When she finally told them, they said it was a terrible mistake. But after the deal closed, they were invited to lunch at my parents' empty little four-room house. While my mother served lunch from a picnic basket and cooler, my father gave them the grand tour. After seeing the home, they changed their tune and told my father that it was a good house, a nice lot, with trees and a driveway too! Best of all, my parents had a home waiting for them after their honeymoon. As soon as you can afford it, buy a home.

Simplify your banking so that you're not paying fees and not focusing on income or how much you have to spend. Focus on expenses. Don't use consumer credit for them. The faster you eliminate old debts, the faster you'll find freedom. Concentrate on your priorities, not on fleeting amusements. Be wary of advertising — buy the bricks, not the fluff.

WORK THE PLAN

There are only two ways to generate savings: earn more and spend less. Of course, doing both is best. Review Chapter 8 for ideas on creating multiple streams of income. After you've exhausted the opportunities for raising your earnings, at least you'll know exactly what your means are.

You'll need to live well below this disposable income level and use your first surplus to establish a positive net worth. That means reducing expenses. Consider how psychological barriers and external conditioning deter you from handling money wisely. It's in many others' best interests to keep you spending and consuming. You must judge the validity of media messages in relation to your own needs, hopes, dreams, and desires. *You* benefit by cutting costs, and remember that you may need to be frugal temporarily until you're free of credit payments. Then you can reward yourself with a luxury purchase, paid for with the money that previously went to your creditors as interest payments. You can adjust your thrift to a more comfortable level at that point too, depending on how fast you want to retire. But you need to base your decision on the ideas in this book. The more suggestions you follow, the faster you'll create wealth, and the faster you'll retire.

When you start handling your money profitably, the surplus, or your savings, will automatically begin to accumulate. These savings should be applied as follows:

(1) **against consumer debts until they're eliminated;**
(2) **as a contribution to your RRSP;**
(3) **to buy adequate housing;**
(4) **to eliminate your mortgage; and**
(5) **to buy wealth-building assets.**

I think I've discussed consumer debt to death, but I really hope you take my suggestions to heart. I'm going to assume you'll make debt elimination the first goal for your savings.

Then you should contribute to an RRSP for three reasons: (1) you'll get a refund or save on the taxes you owe, (2) you'll establish your nest egg for your conventional retirement years, and (3) you can treat your initial contributions as an emergency fund. I recommend depositing an amount equal to six months' expenses for emergencies, an amount that shouldn't be exorbitant once you overhaul your spending behaviour and get rid of your debts. Of course, the amount that you can contribute will be restricted by how much you're allowed to put into your RRSP and by the amount of surplus you have to work with. Regardless, it should be placed in a cashable, conservative, registered investment. Hopefully, by holding it in your RRSP, you'll be less tempted to use it for nonemergencies. You'll also be able to enjoy the cash refund on that year's tax filing and the future tax-free growth while the money remains in the plan. Be sure to make the full contribution as soon as possible, and then get the forms from Canada Customs and Revenue Agency to apply for a reduction in your income tax taken off at source.

Once you have your emergency fund, you'll need to decide how to split the surplus for additional RRSP contributions and mortgage payments. It really depends on your situation. How much you already have in your RRSP, how much you'll need, how many years until your conventional retirement — these issues will need to be addressed. As well, you need to look at the other investment options for your RRSP once you have enough conservative holdings. Ask, ask, ask. Consult with advisors, naturally, but do your own research as well. Take another look at Chapter 7.

As far as I'm concerned, the sooner you discharge your mortgage the better. Even if you have a low interest rate, if you keep making payments over the next 20 years, you could easily pay more in total interest by the end than if you have a higher rate of interest but pay off the mortgage over a shorter term. Do the math. You'll also be restricted by the terms of your mortgage in paying it down faster. Talk to your mortgage lender, discuss alternatives, read some books, do some research at other lenders, and then decide for yourself. Paying down your mortgage, though, will still depend on how much you can regularly expect to have in savings and how much you're allowed to or need to put into your RRSP.

Then, after you've indulged in a priority luxury and still have some savings, it's time to research nonregistered investment opportunities. There are so many books, media shows, and advisors in the area of investing that you can spend a great deal of time and effort gathering the knowledge necessary to make the best decisions. If investing isn't an interest or hobby of yours, read a few articles on how to choose a financial planner, paying particular attention to any bias the author or organization may have. You could visit the Financial Planners Standards Council web site at www.cfp-ca.org or the Canadian Association of Financial Planners site at www.cafp.org; both sites offer advice on finding a planner. Even so, you must understand the various financial products available to make an informed decision. You should feel comfortable with your investments and think that you have the best combination of products to suit your own needs and risk tolerance.

I suggest that you interview a number of advisors and ask

every question you can think of, but don't make a commitment to one on the spot. Rank those who made you feel the most confident, and after a week or so visit the contenders again, still avoiding a final decision. The reason for the second meeting is to confirm your initial impressions. Then, if you decide on a couple of commissioned salespeople, divide your investment money equally between them and monitor the progress of their products quarterly. When a year has gone by, judge the results of each asset class in your portfolio against competitors' similar investments and compare overall market sector results. Financial newspapers publish summarized charts for that purpose.

Before I began actively investing in the stock market, I went to an investment house and told the planner that he'd receive only half of my money since I wanted to compare the return I'd make on my own with the results from his choice of experts. He didn't like the idea, so he didn't get my money. At another firm, the broker said he'd rather handle all of my money but was happy to look after half of it. By the end of the year, I'd made a better profit from my own investment decisions, so I transferred my money from the broker to my existing account with a discount brokerage, and I've kept it there ever since.

I spend a lot of time on investment research, but if that doesn't appeal to you, make the effort to find good financial advisors, and periodically check your portfolio's performance thereafter.

As you practise living below your means, your assets should grow steadily from the regular infusion of savings and investment profits. You should also have a good idea of your average costs of living and therefore be able to predict the amount of income required to cover future costs. The projection won't be precise, but in my experience it's been close.

When you're making your projections, consider if you want to leave money for your heirs, because any inheritance will affect how much you'll need for your retirement after 65. From the date you want to retire early until age 65, you'll need only enough to cover your estimated future costs from your nest egg's original capital and return. Count on both the original investment and its return being used up by the time you're 65. It means you'll likely use a different formula for each retirement period to calculate the correct nest egg amount. This is where a good financial advisor can help. Find one who will perform the calculations based on what *you* suggest the variables should be.

As you approach your target date, the economic conditions at that time will provide a good indication of the variables you'll have to assume in figuring out how much you'll need in each portfolio. You'll have a better approximation of interest rates, investment performance, and inflation rates. Then all you'll have to do is provide your advisor with the following variables: the level of income required for early retirement and regular retirement, the time span of each, if the capital is to be used up, and the estimated rates for inflation and investment returns based on government economic data and your personal economic data. You could also use one of the many financial software programs that offer retirement planning, either bought at retail or found on the Internet. Be careful, though, that the program asks for all of the variables and doesn't assume fixed numbers that might not accurately reflect your circumstances. For example, you should be able to insert your desired level of net income in retirement (expressed in current dollars), and you should agree with or be able to change any figures the equation uses for inflation rate or investment return. You also need to consider if you'll have pension benefits, a RRIF, and/or annuity, for your conventional retirement period. This is a complex area involving many personal decisions, so you really need to speak to a knowledgeable advisor.

Don't forget, if you miscalculate or something unforeseen happens during your early retirement, you'll probably only need to make a temporary adjustment or take a temporary job. But before you reach early retirement, as you're trying to cut costs, know that the temporary pain will afford an exceptional gain. Then, no matter what happens later, you'll have learned sound money-handling skills, which is an accomplishment in itself.

More than likely, though, you'll work at something in retirement that you've always wanted to do, and it may generate some income. Even though I believe I have enough in my RRSP, I still make contributions to it to lower my income to the non-taxable level when needed, and the extra funds in my registered plan are like having insurance. I can also carry forward the RRSP deductions to be used against income in future years, and in the meantime my portfolio continues to grow with the contributions earning a tax-free return inside the plan.

When your Balance Sheet reflects a healthy net worth, you'll already know freedom. You'll have options. Wealth does that for you. Then, when you no longer have to work, you might think that your job isn't so bad after all. The stress of needing a job will be gone, and you can decide what form early retirement will take. Without the pressure of worrying about "the job," it'll be easier to gain perspective on the really important things in your life.

From beginning to end, though, you have to be three things: a dreamer, driven, and determined. You need to be a dreamer to picture what you want and see yourself achieving it. You have to be driven, which means making a promise to yourself and following through with the action to get what you want. You must be determined to overcome adversity and persevere until you reach your goal. That's why I think almost anyone can do what I've done. But not without dreams, drive, and determination.

Many people have asked me if I ever thought I'd become an author. Honestly, no. I hadn't planned on it. But when I decided to just go ahead and begin writing, it got done. It reminds me of my favourite landmark on the way to my parents' summer house. There's a lovely farm with rolling hills and a century home with gingerbread trim set across from a big red barn. Painted on the side of the barn in tall white letters are the words "Neverthought Farm." It's amazing how many wonderful things can happen that ordinarily you wouldn't expect. You don't know what you can do until you try. Sure! Why not? Don't let anyone else tell you otherwise. You can find financial freedom if you want it. Do the math. Make a plan. Then take action. Persevere, and realize your dreams.